ANNIE MORRIS

WHEN A HAPPY THING FALLS

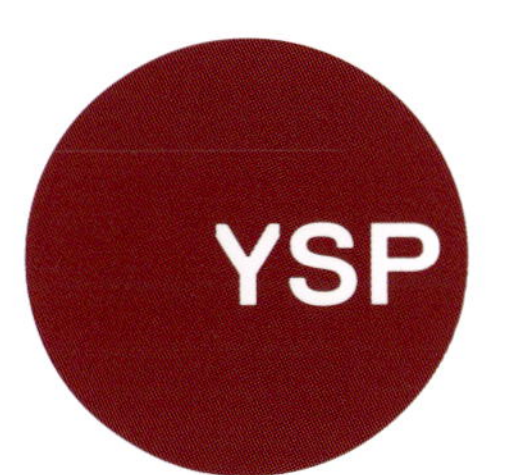

CONTENTS

Next page: Annie Morris in her studio, 2021. Photograph Idris Khan

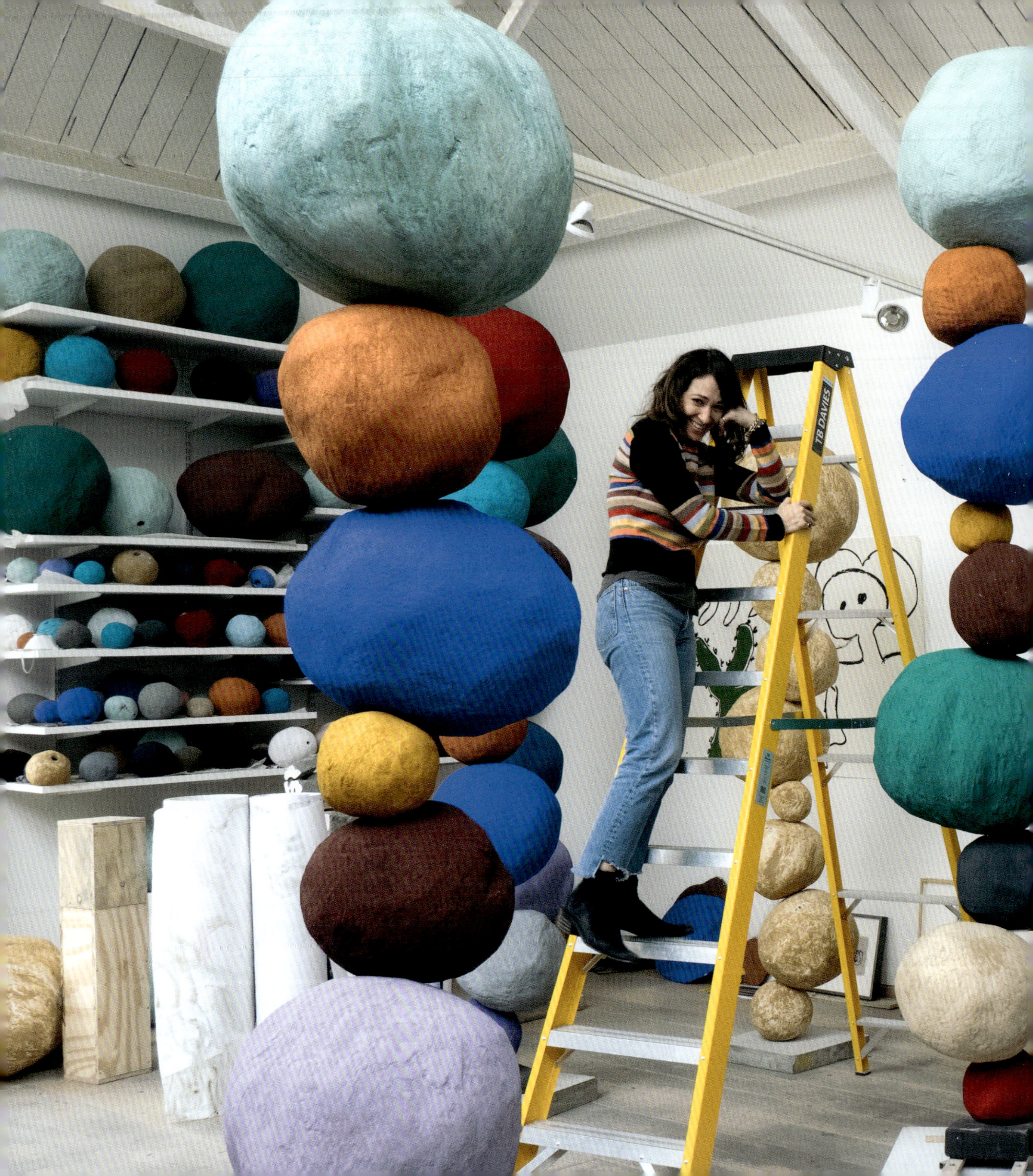

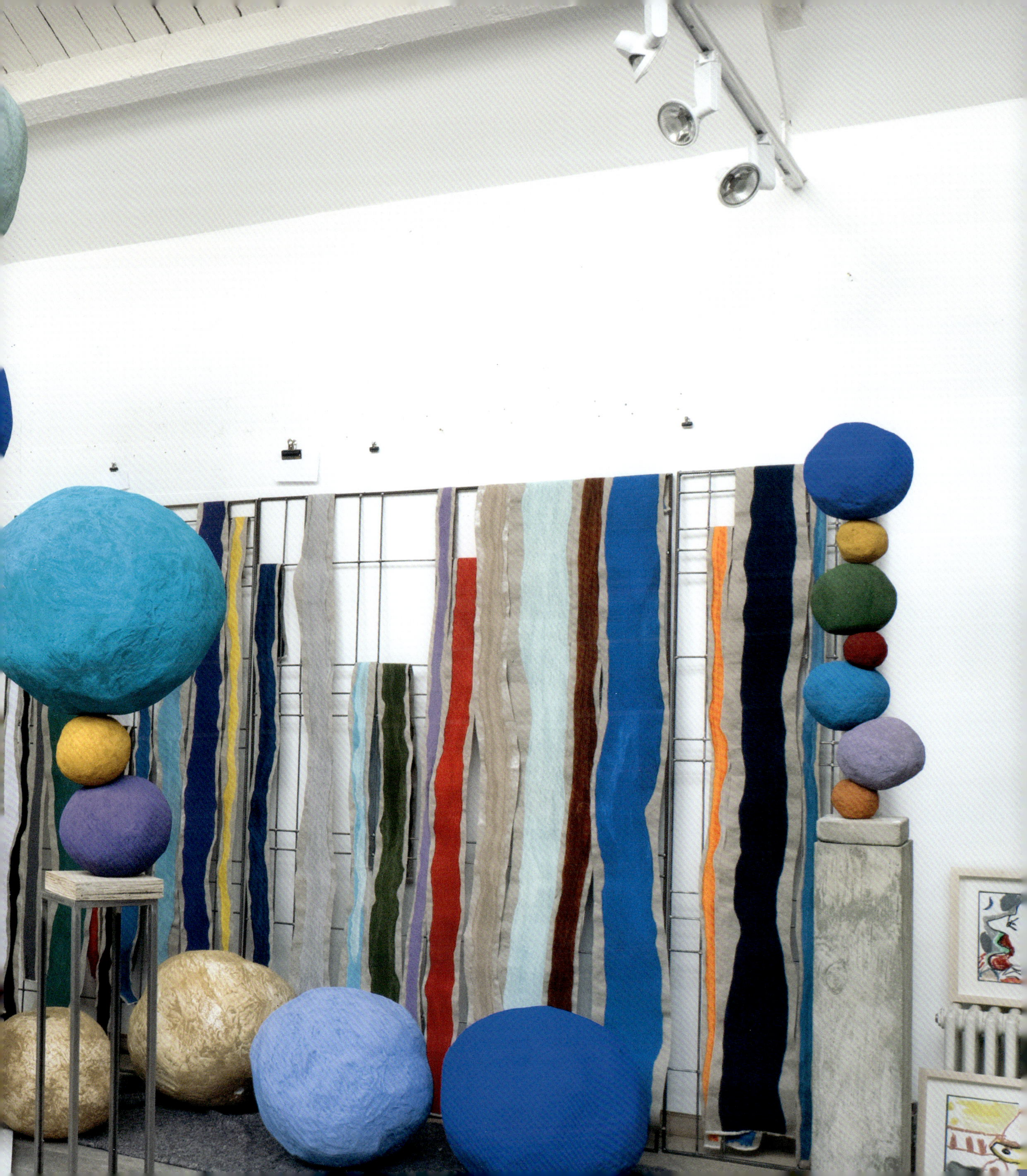

FOREWORD

For two generations, Yorkshire Sculpture Park has been a place where life has played out within an often-otherworldly environment. Families, friends, strangers and communities come together in wonder, intrigue and energetic exchange. Day by day, year by year, we witness modern and contemporary art playing an extraordinary part in people's lives and see how nature and landscape give richness and vitality to life. YSP offers sanctuary, friendship, hope, and vision for all people. For artists it is a never-ending resource and stimulation. The Weston was born from a desire to create an eastern entrance into the Park, enabling a very different and beautiful entry into this 18th-century landscape. The light-filled building forms an inspirational gateway and the Weston Gallery programme emphasises the importance of human contact and of creativity. Projects here connect people through the senses, through interaction and through contemplation. Encompassing difference and variety, they stimulate empathy and positive change.

Annie Morris began her *Stack* series in 2014. These works result from her grief following the stillbirth of her first child. The tragedy catalysed a compulsion for her to draw intense, dense circular forms and then to make irregular spheres that seem swollen and fecund – like brightly coloured fruits. The gallery works are sculpted in plaster and sand, and painted with carefully sourced, raw pigments in vivid hues such as ultramarine, viridian and ochre. Her outdoor sculptures are cast in bronze with similarly rich, vibrant colours burned into their surfaces, often in many layers. The globe forms are arranged into columns, some short, some tall, all seemingly precariously off-balance.

The totem is probably the earliest form of communal sculpture, with the three-metre-high wooden *Shigir Idol* in Russia as our earliest known work of ritual art, made 12,000 years ago at the end of the Ice Age. Upright forms are found in every indigenous culture across human time, tracing cultural beliefs and legends and implying that the making of objects and symbols of emotional value is intrinsic to human development. Most of us have watched a child stack blocks or rings to make a tower and on a pebbly beach, you're likely to come across a teetering stack of carefully chosen stones. At a time of almost unbearable sorrow, Morris understood the urgency of hope and was compelled to make upright forms that are both unstable and bursting with colour and life. Pigments and paint grinding equipment made around 350,000 years ago have been found near Lusaka in Zambia and through pigment, too, Annie connects with the prehistoric social practice of forming shapes with minerals which, although natural, required significant effort to obtain, grind to a powder and mix with an agent to create early paint. Probably ochre, derived from iron oxide, was the first colour to be used – as body paint and on the walls of caves, as well as carbon black from charred wood. In the 6th and 7th centuries CE true ultramarine was used in Afghani Buddhist and Zoroastrian cave temples – it is the most expensive of pigments, made by grinding lapis lazuli. In ancient Egypt, the first synthetic pigment called Egyptian blue was created by heating quartz sand, lime and malachite and later it was intensively used in Roman Pompeii and Herculaneum. Raw and burnt sienna and raw and burnt umber indicate the places at which the minerals were mined, while Indian yellow was collected from the urine of cattle fed on mango leaves and vermilion made by grinding natural cinnabar.

The impulse to make art is essential to humankind. In both method and colour, in intent and realisation, Morris intuitively connects with ancient practices of art/making and thereby extends the trajectory of human ingenuity and compulsion to create art. Emphatically independent, Morris's careful, instinctive colour combinations – shown here as a forest of sculpture – create a mesmerising installation that is as alive as it is vivid. These are brave works, each one singing to its own tune, and collectively forming a chorus. We pay tribute to this exceptional artist for the depth of her statement and for bringing such a vibrant and heartfelt expression of hope and beauty to Yorkshire Sculpture Park.

We are very grateful to the team who prepared and installed *When a Happy Thing Falls*, including Annie's studio colleagues Ailbhe Murphy, Paula Morison, Julie Smith, Jon Doubleday, Evan Thomas and Anna Brooke as well as the YSP Technical and Curatorial teams. I would like to thank Emma Spencer in the YSP Learning Team for her sensitive and vital related work with families who have experienced grief and Helen Pheby for initiating the project and bringing to it her customary care and intelligence. Nothing at YSP is possible without core funding from Arts Council England, Wakefield Council, the Liz and Terry Bramall Foundation, the Sakana Foundation and Roger Evans, to all of whom I extend our thanks. We are very grateful to Catherine Loewe and David Trigg for their texts which so incisively amplify Annie's work. Most importantly, we are indebted to Annie Morris for giving so much of herself to this exhibition and for sharing her family of work with us all. She in turn wishes to thank her husband Idris Khan and her mother for their incredible support.

Clare Lilley, YSP Director of Programme

INTRODUCTION

When a Happy Thing Falls in the Weston Gallery at Yorkshire Sculpture Park is Annie Morris's first UK museum solo show. Although the sculptures and tapestries were all made in the last four years, the installation has the character of an art historical exhibition because her work is fundamentally concerned with the core principles of art: line, form and colour. Her sculpture stacks bring to mind the palette of artists who have gone before, such as that Leonardo da Vinci held as he painted *The Virgin of the Rocks* for example. Morris has spoken often of the profound inspiration she derives from pigment, of spending hours in the art supply shop Sennelier near to the École des Beaux-Arts where she studied in Paris, determined to find ways to embody the array of colours in drawer after drawer of wax and other crayons, paints and pastels – the shop being famous for inventing oil pastels for Pablo Picasso. She experimented with different ways to capture the pigment in stasis, to preserve its raw, visceral colour undiluted, such as flinging paints onto canvases prepared with linseed oil.

Colour and creativity are at the heart of human development. To me, children seem to delight in the gloop of pigment-rich paints, mark making with their fingers and hands, smearing their faces in primary stripes. Bright colours are associated with fun, joy and happiness. In Morris's hands they are matured by the patina of lived experience. Art is an expression of life, the full experience of which includes profound grief as well as joy, love lost as well as found, periods when the world seems monochrome not full colour. After a deeply traumatic and tragic event, Morris's first response was to draw in biro, using the point of the pen to channel grief at the loss of a child at nearly full term as well as the death of her mother-in-law. She continues to mark make in this way, often with sewn rather than drawn lines, at the start of working each day. The lines reflected the shape of her own pregnant body, a simple black figure on fabric, each slightly different with straight lines of hair that later fed into abstract grid works. After a time she introduced coloured lines above the belly, representing hope and that some light was being let back in. These lines have evolved into the stacked sculptures for which Morris has become especially well known. Each starts life as a watercolour, complete when she is happy with the balance of colour and form. The sculpture elements are then carved from a ball of plaster, prepared with sand in a unique process developed by the artist, to which the different pigments adhere. Over many years Morris has learned the characteristics of different pigments and how to capture their essence. For example, the Weston Gallery installation includes *Stack 3, Terre Verte* (2021), featuring a vibrant purple for the first time. *When a Happy Thing Falls* includes both Morris's first and most recent bronze sculptures, whose coloured surfaces are the result of burning pigment into the surface in many layers. Another edition of the most recent bronze sculpture *Stack 9, Ultramarine Blue* (2020-21) is being shown simultaneously at Frieze Sculpture Park, London, selected by Clare Lilley, YSP Director of Programme – making family connections across the country.

Morris chose YSP for her first museum show, partly because of its stunning landscape setting and the opportunity to appreciate her work in relation to this backdrop, but also because it is home to the long-term loan of *The Family of Man* (1970) by Barbara Hepworth. The last major piece made before she died, the installation comprises a group of nine, exquisitely patinated bronze figures, ranging from *Youth* and *Young Girl* through *Bride* and *Bridegroom*, *Parent I* and *Parent II, Grandparent I* and *Grandparent II* to the *Ultimate Form* or *Ancestor* at the top of the hill. Inspired by childhood experiences of seeing figures in the Yorkshire landscape, it is testament to Hepworth's wishes for there to be a permanent sculpture park in the UK that the work is here for people to enjoy. Routinely conserved by Laura Davies, a specialist in Hepworth's patinas, particular areas of the sculptures are a rich azure, echoing the sea around St Ives where Hepworth moved to in 1939. These figures very definitely inhabit their area of YSP; on a cold day they seem introverted and stoic, on a warm day almost golden and inviting. They have individual personalities but family resemblances.

Morris has shared her own family of work with YSP, each unique but with motifs that run through the tapestries and sculptures. The Yorkshire-born art critic Sir Herbert Read said that each artwork is unique to the person experiencing it depending on what they have lived through. Morris has harnessed her exceptional talent and assimilated her experiences to express what it means to live a life. To encounter her work is immediately exhilarating, our eyes and emotions following the upward lift of the sculptures. As the layers of meaning are understood, and people bring their own experiences into the dynamic, the full spectrum of humanity is revealed – the compensation for growing old being our memories, the price of love being grief, the times of monochrome making our appreciation of the joyful all the more colourful.

Helen Pheby PhD, YSP Head of Curatorial Programme

Next page: *There is a Land Called Loss* 2011-12, oil, gouache, pen and ink on paper. Photograph Steve White

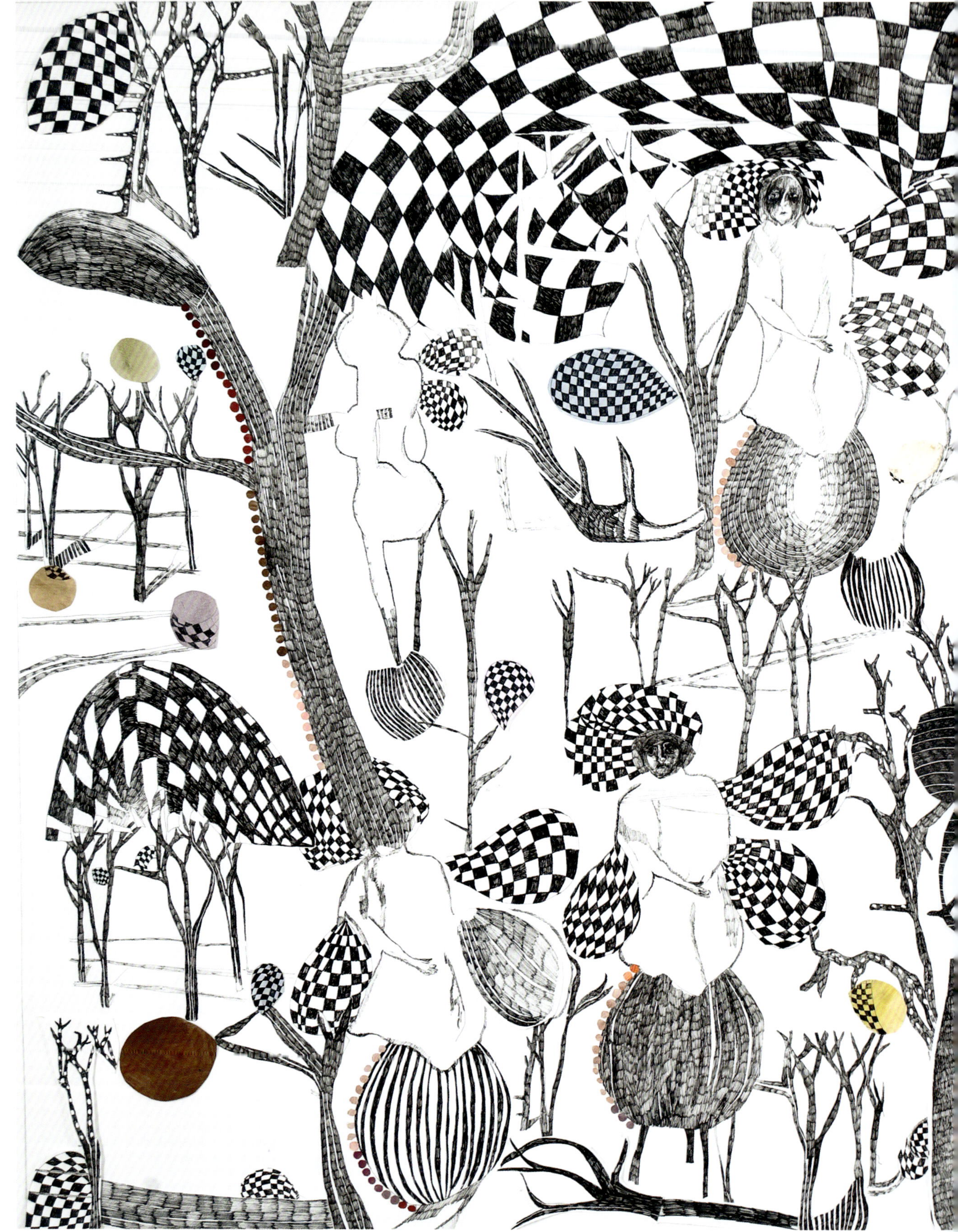

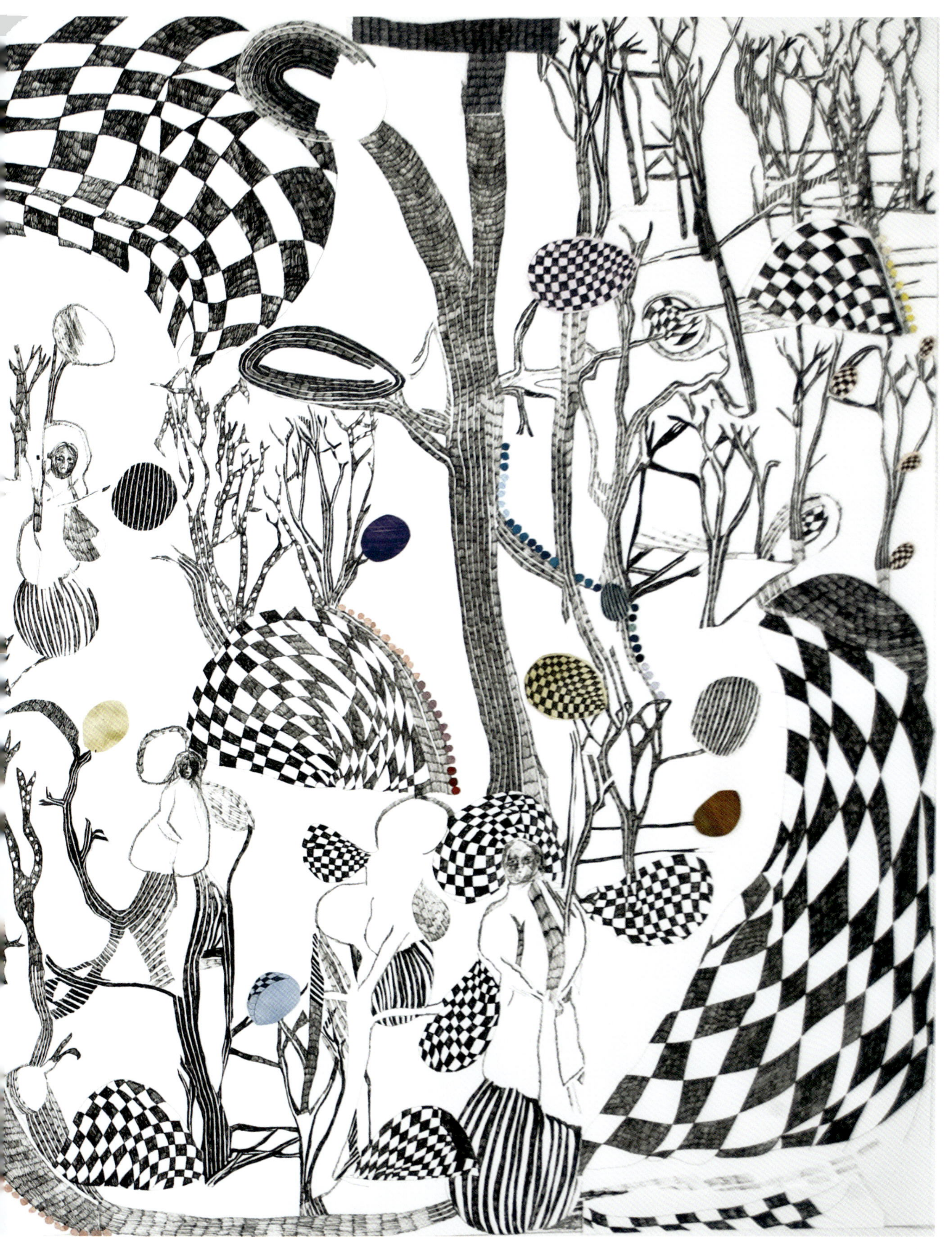

WHEN A HAPPY THING FALLS

The first impression of Annie Morris's work on entering her North London studio is of a soaring forest of colours, created by her vibrant sculptures with plaster, sand and using raw pigments in jewel-like hues of cobalt blue, cadmium red, viridian green, sharp turquoise and ochre. The immersive experience of Morris's studio practice is re-created in the Weston Gallery at Yorkshire Sculpture Park, where the sculptures appear to be in conversation with each other. Crafted in the shape of a three-dimensional artist's palette, these sculptures are infused with both strength and vulnerability, carrying the tremulous joy of expectant promise. Morris's gravity-defying forms are poignant metaphors of the ability to conquer the impossible, testament to the vibrancy of life which can nevertheless seem like an endless balancing act. This sense of precariousness, a condition that could topple into chaos at any moment, resonates on many levels and feels particularly prescient in the anxiety-ridden times we are all living through. Morris says, 'I became obsessed with the round shape that my body took on during my first pregnancy. When it was taken away from me so suddenly, I wanted it back, so I would draw it every day'.[1]

In Morris's practice everything begins from drawing, a medium she works fervently in, making hundreds of sketches daily using various materials including pen, crayon, pencil, oil-stick, watercolour and pastel which often lead to making large scale hand sewn tapestries. The sewn works on raw linen which line the Weston Gallery arose from a desire to transform her sharp, fast and fragile marks into something slower, tactile and permanent, recreating the beautiful chalk effect with numerous animated lines of stitching. This series depicts the recurring figure of a reclining woman with arched back and prominent breast, her scribbly sculptural-like hair replacing facial features as a means of emotive expression. Both archetypal and highly personal, the figure is always seen with small lines of colour hovering above her. This idea was originally inspired by a 1988 painting by Antoni Tàpies called *Bed with Colour*, a brown sketchy bed with small rainbow lines above it. The bed is intimate and domestic, a potent symbol of sleep, dreams, sex, birth and death, but what struck Morris was the suggestion of separating colour and keeping the pure pigments together. Morris tells me, 'The coloured lines were almost like a key to what could be, I took those little lines and the condensation of colour became these sculptural pieces. I was looking so much at the lines and feeling comforted by them, so I wanted to expand on that, the way they have such a lot of power, essentially they

   [1] Interview with Annie Morris by the author, February 2020

say the same thing as the sculptures'.[2] Above all, those multi-coloured hovering marks represented a feeling of hope, the suggestion that something could potentially happen, which is why we are now standing in a room brimming with colour.

Abstract planes of colour have long been the domain of painting, so it is extraordinary to see sculptures that physicalise colour in such a visceral way. Morris refers to Rauschenberg's deeply autobiographical work of 1955 entitled *Bed* and the almost shocking way in which he splashed paint samples onto his sheets and quilt, creating the first of his radical *Combines*. Despite being situated in the messy, liminal state between life and art, there remains something extremely poignant about the colour palette as a fundamental medium through which artists speak. Morris's works also appear to be situated between the idea and the thing, acting as midwives to their own next form — allowing her sculpture to be seen as 3D paintings and the work on fabric as sculptural, namely in the thread paintings and her enigmatic series of works made of curvy coloured strips of canvas hung on metal grids.

While Morris finds inspiration from her travels around the world, like the explosive multicoloured powder paints of Holi — the Hindu 'festival of colours' which celebrates the eternal and divine love of Radha and Krishna — her obsession with colour started as a student in Paris studying at the École des Beaux-Arts under Giuseppe Penone, 'I was interested in pigment in purest sense, inspired by going to art shops and looking at raw colours. There is a particular store in Paris where Picasso used to buy his materials called *Sennelier*, which was right next to the Beaux Arts. It's the kind of shop where if you're interested, they'd open drawers and there would be every shade of burnt umber and every shade of yellow ochre, colours that you simply could not believe'.[3] This is the marchand de couleurs made famous for producing the finest pigments for countless pioneers in the use of colour including Sisley, Degas, Bonnard, Soutine, Gauguin and Picasso. Morris mixed her own colours, which she would throw at her canvases, always looking to keep the vibrancy alive, experimenting with materials in the search for a way to create a texture that looked as if it could never dry. She says, 'what was interesting in the drying process was that something beautiful happened, the pigment started to dry but it stayed absolutely like velvet on the surface of the canvas'.[4]

Morris has since been continuously drawn to layered textures, the move to a much larger studio enabling her to cast sculpture in bronze, experimenting with ways of burning pigments and nitrates into the material. Working in bronze for many years has been both challenging and rewarding, as with the latest series Morris

[2] Interview with Annie Morris by the author, August 2021
[3] Interview with Annie Morris by the author, February 2020
[4] Ibid.

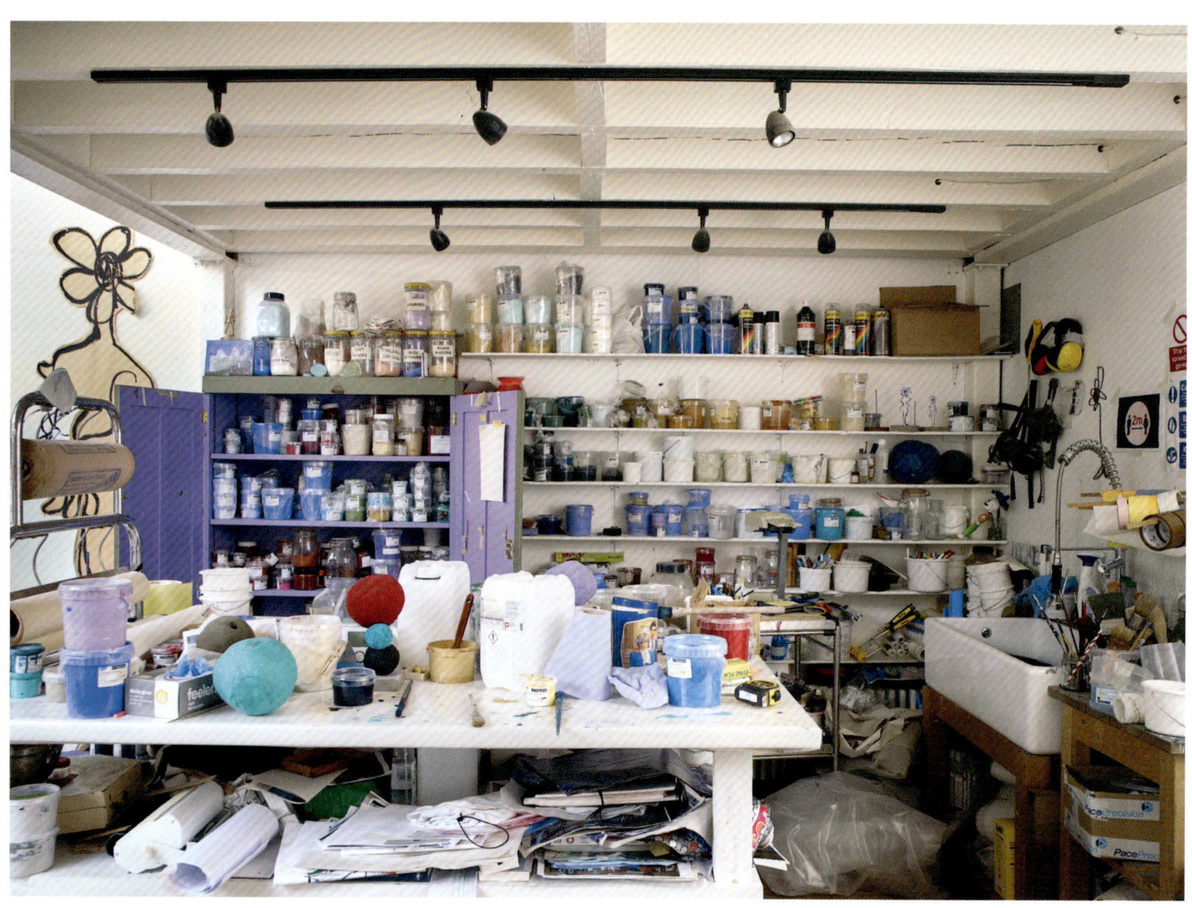

14   Annie Morris studio, 2021. Photograph Steve White

has honed into a much more resolved technique to texture the surface of the material, seeking a similar effect to the pigment works, a feat almost impossible to achieve in bronze. She has developed a unique layering process with the pigment burnt into the bronze, adding up to ten layers of paint onto the bronze and mixing different colours to achieve the distinctive thick texture and luminous depth to spectacular, jewel-like effect. 'I adore the copper blue as it feels like unearthing a large lapis lazuli stone, it has that semi-precious quality.'[5]

Colour is often seen as almost subversive, especially in monumental bronze, so this work is particularly groundbreaking, creating something truly permanent that Morris has always yearned to do. 'Bronze is such an extraordinary material that it is normally left as it is with its natural patina, so it feels like breaking the rules to paint something that is already so exquisite.'[6] The bronze stack displayed outside the Weston Gallery is one of Morris's largest sculptures to date and she is working on one that promises to be truly epic. Historically, not many sculptors, let alone women, have tackled the use of colour at scale, but Niki de Saint Phalle must be the exception. For Morris she is hugely influential, not only for her exuberant use of colour (with a nod to Miró, Matisse and Chagall) but also for her ecstatic, whimsical worlds with a dark and mythic edge. Both feminine and feminist, she drew on a troubled relationship with her father to create a lexicon of archetypal characters – her iconic *Nanas*, animals and monsters.

Carl Jung described colour as 'the mother tongue of the subconscious'[7] and it is from this primordial place where inner emotion takes outward form that Morris's use of colour emanates. It is well known that the wavelengths of light we see as colour are converted into electrical impulses that pass through the part of the brain where our emotions deliver responses. We don't just see colours we 'feel', even taste, hear and smell them too. Morris's colours thus function on a raw emotional level as triggers for memories, often conveying conflicting emotions of joy and pain, love and loss. It is as if Morris has filled the big black hole with rainbow colours and in the process replaced despair with hope. Morris's symbolic imagery refers to the cycle of life, death and rebirth, in which everything seems rotund, fecund and earthy. Yet there is a palpable sense of working through disturbing psychological events with recurring motifs such as the *Flower Headed Woman*, the curvy silhouette that appears everywhere in freestanding steel sculptures, drawings and stitched textiles. Embroidery carries domestic references – girls need to know how to sew and mend – but the tradition is steeped in history and myth from the narrative power of the Bayeux tapestry, to the mythological Penelope in the *Odyssey*, her fate inextricably bound to the fabric she is weaving. Morris's

[5] Interview with Annie Morris by the author, February 2020
[6] Ibid.
[7] Carl Jung, 'Uber die Archetypen des kollektiven Unbewussten' in *Eranos-Jahrbuch* Zurich, 1934, np

devotional, laborious stitching is a poignant form of healing and renewal that commits the fleeting idea or feeling to perpetuity. There is an elegiac aspect to her work reflecting on the beautiful but transient nature of life, she says: 'The theme is both loss and hope for me and this show will be full of delight, but I feel as if each sculpture commemorates someone who might have died, so in a sense it is about both life and death.'[8] Morris invokes the spirit of the great pioneer Barbara Hepworth, who famously loved carving her distinctive round and organic shapes. Her powerful bronze series of nine sculptures *The Family of Man* (1970), one of the last major works completed before her death, is here at Yorkshire Sculpture Park. Representing the stages of human life and resembling ancient monuments, their stacked and abstracted forms are imbued with a sense of remembrance that seems intrinsically connected to Morris's work.

Morris has created a personal language in which life and art coalesce, distilled through the complex emotions and searing experiences of being a woman, daughter, sister, wife and mother. Her fluid, instinctive creative process is as much the bearer of meaning as the emotive subject or form, slipping between the rule-bound spaces of painting and sculpture, abstraction and figuration. Whether using biro or bronze, Morris's vibrant work oscillates between the personal and collective memory, enmeshed in glorious, life-affirming colour.

'Love was a feeling completely bound up with colour,
like thousands of rainbows superimposed one on top of the other.' Paulo Coelho

Catherine Loewe

 ⁸ Interview with Annie Morris by the author, August 2021

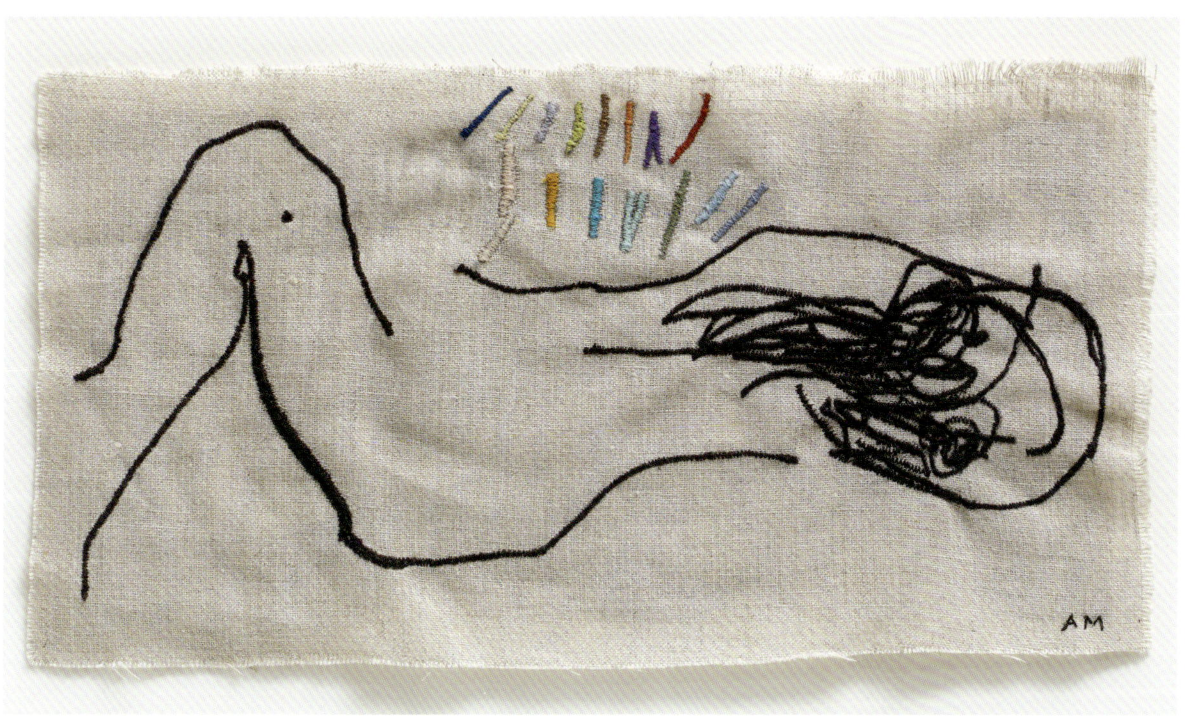

Woman with colour, 2015, thread on linen canvas. Photograph Steve White
Next page: Annie Morris studio. Photograph Steve White

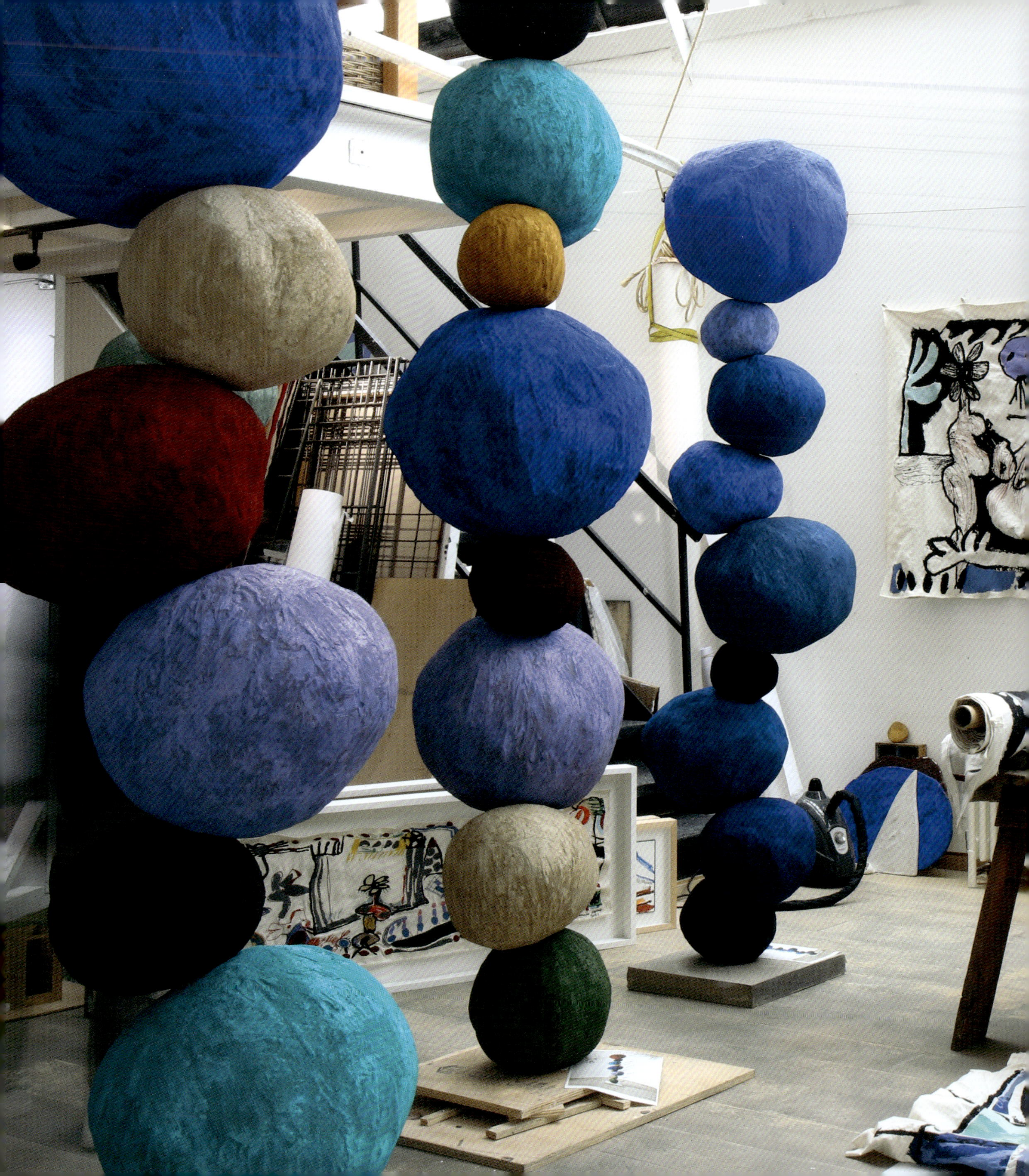

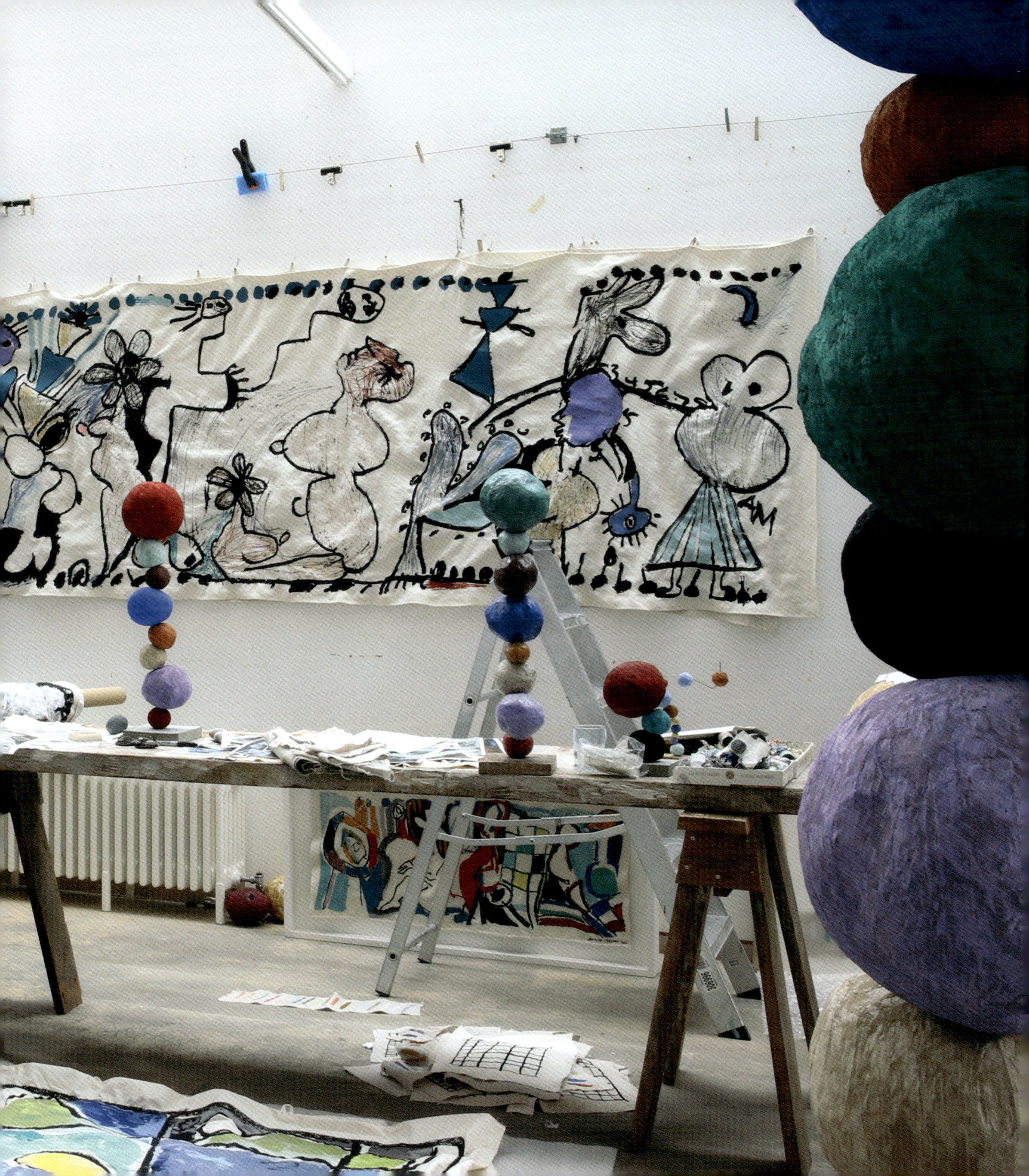

EXHIBITION PHOTOGRAPHY

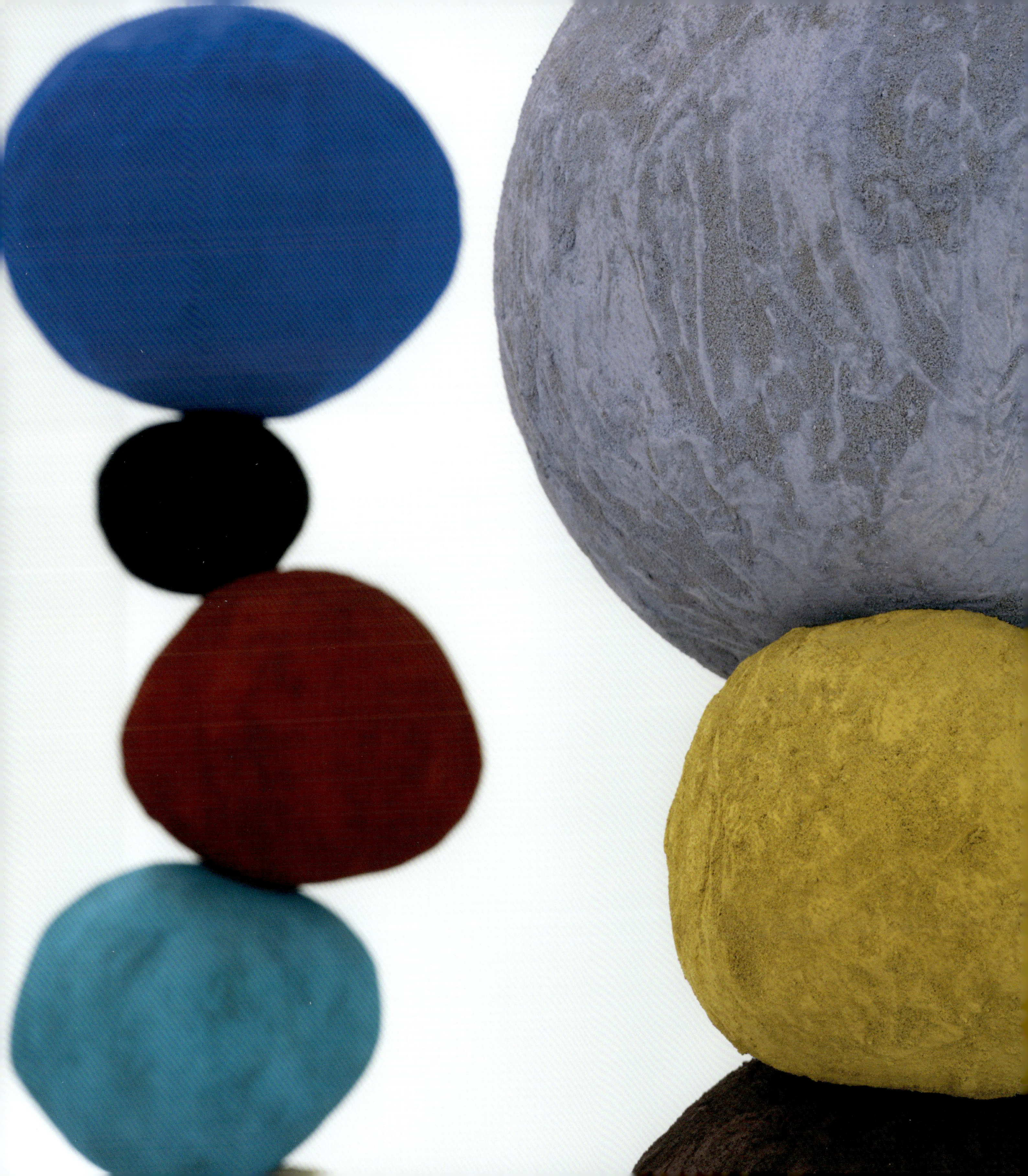

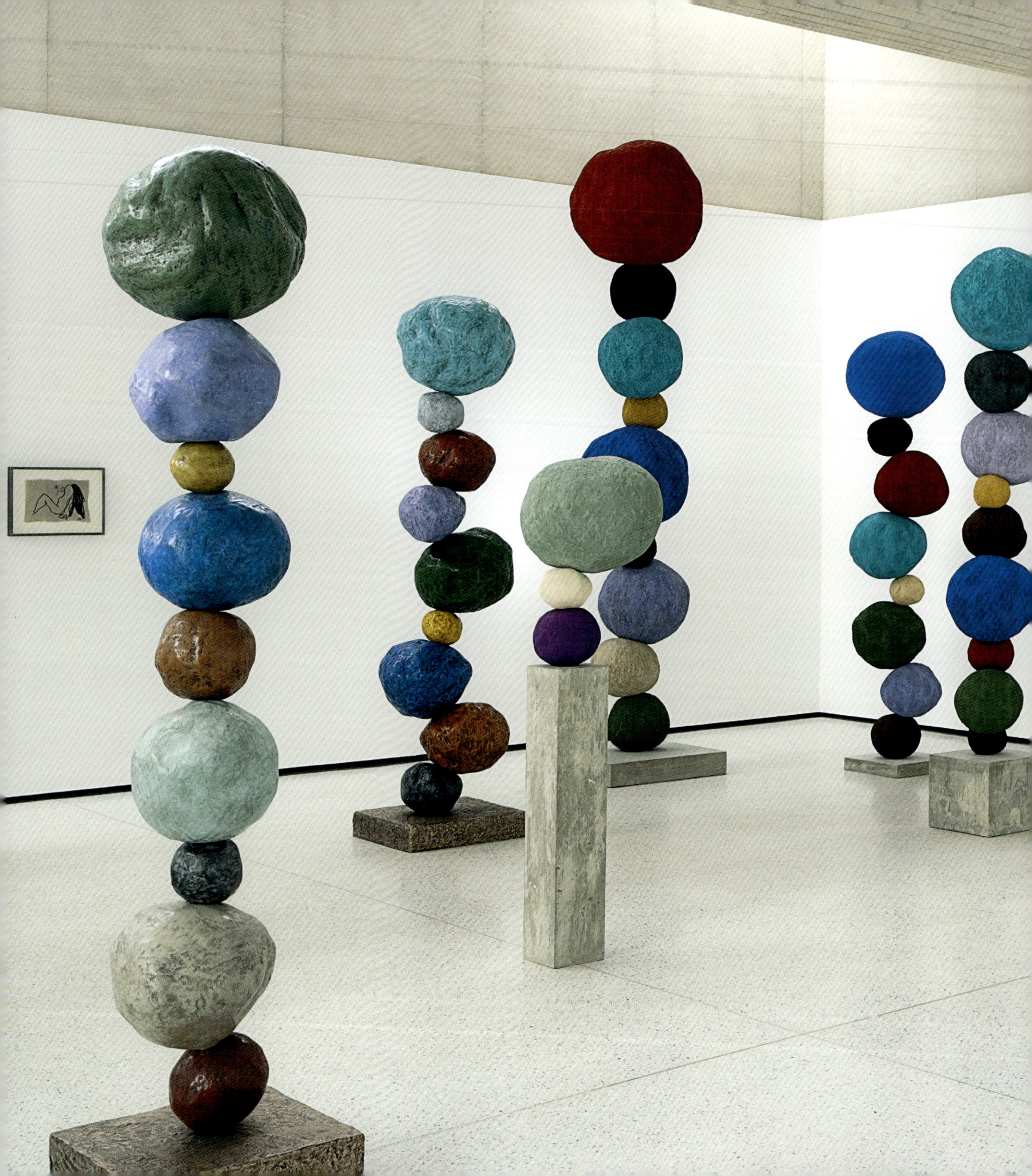

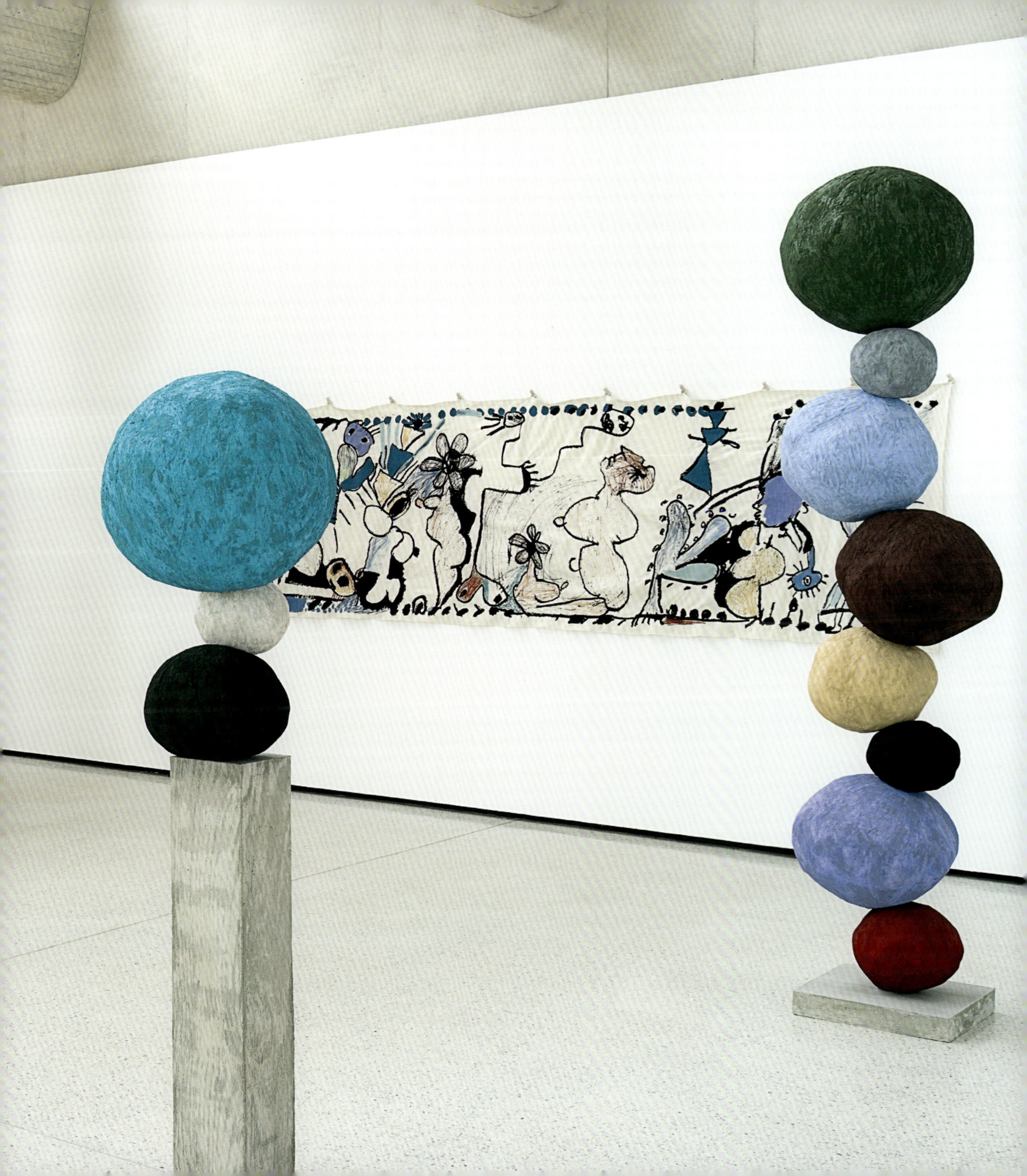

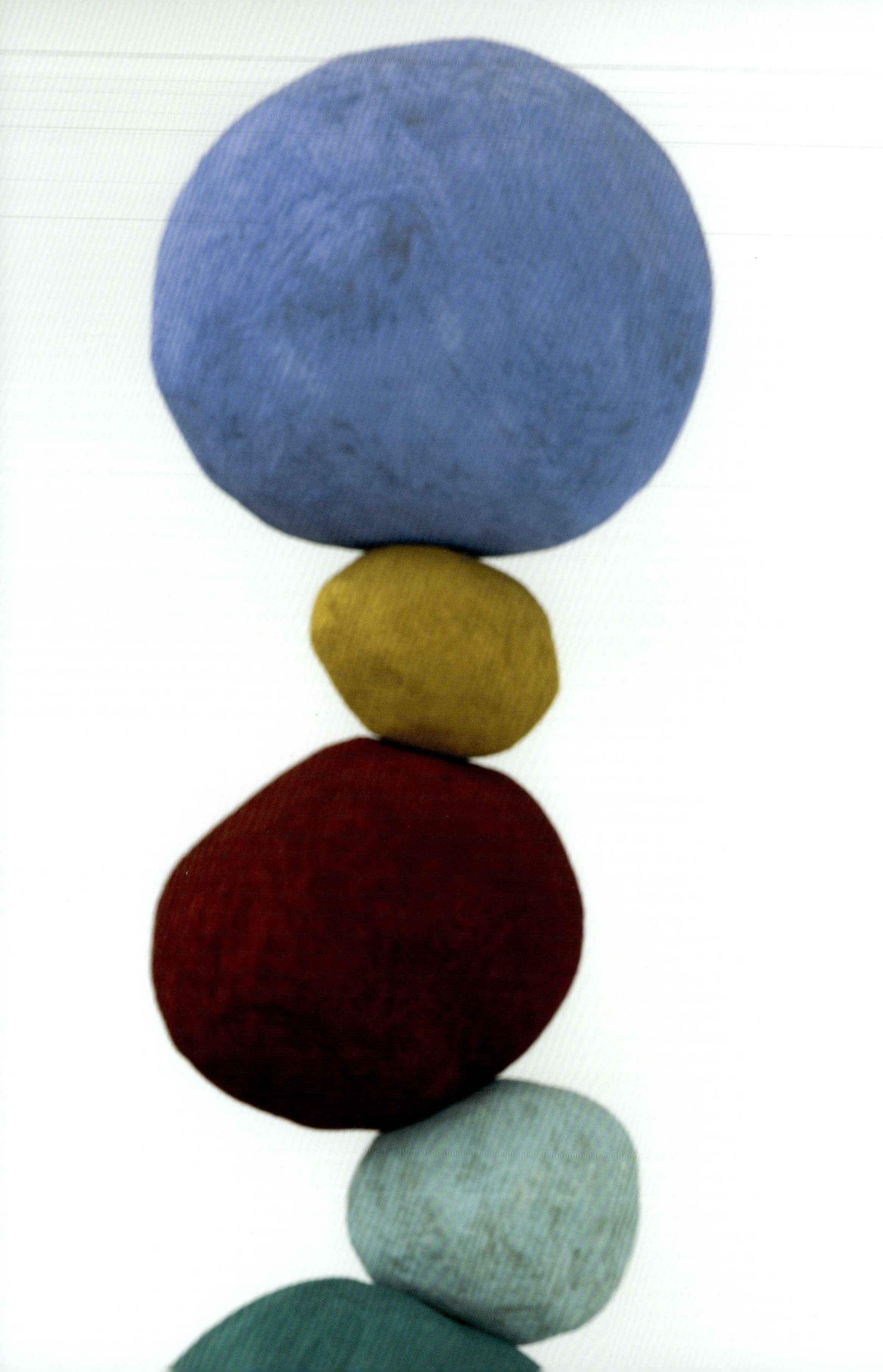

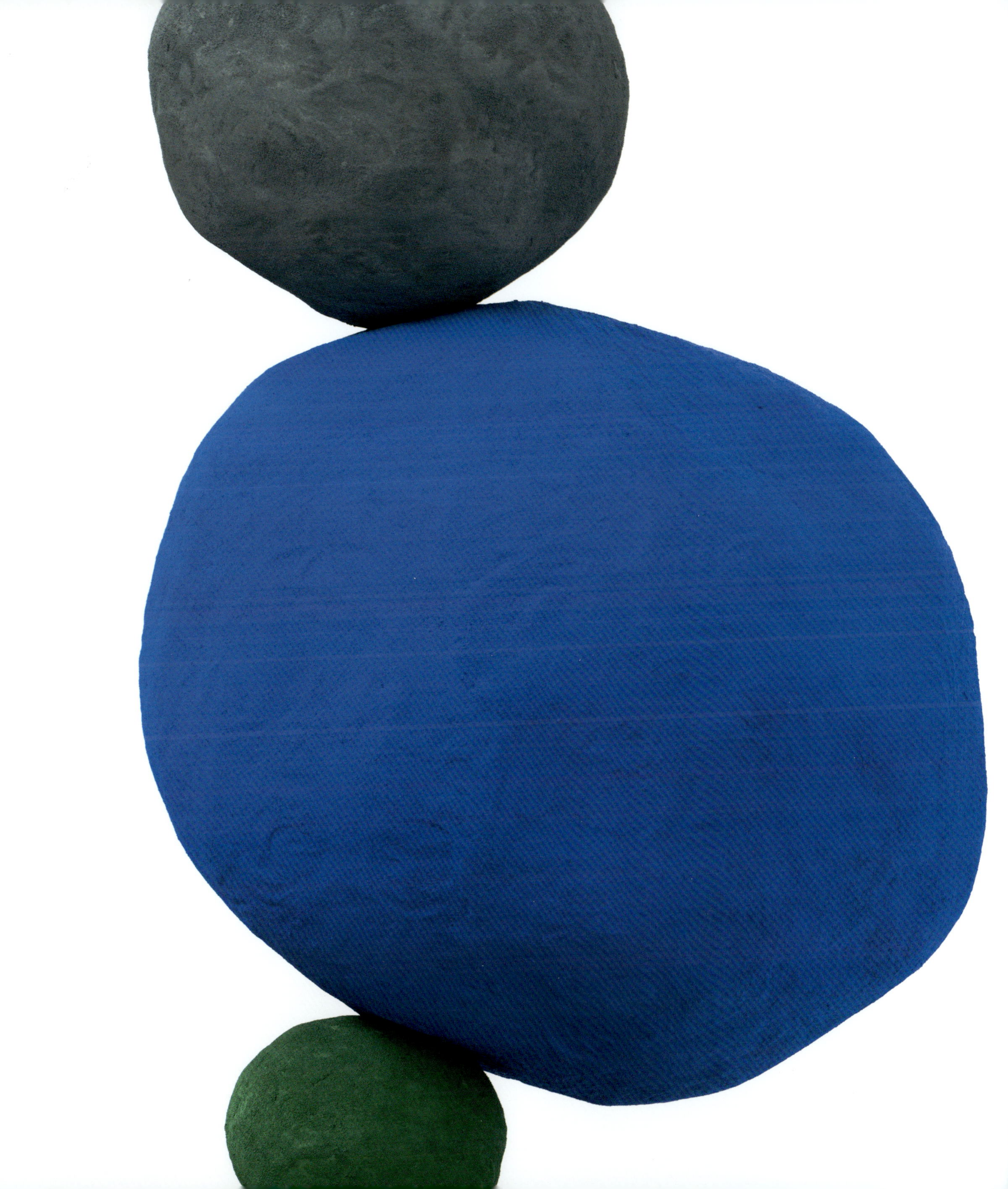

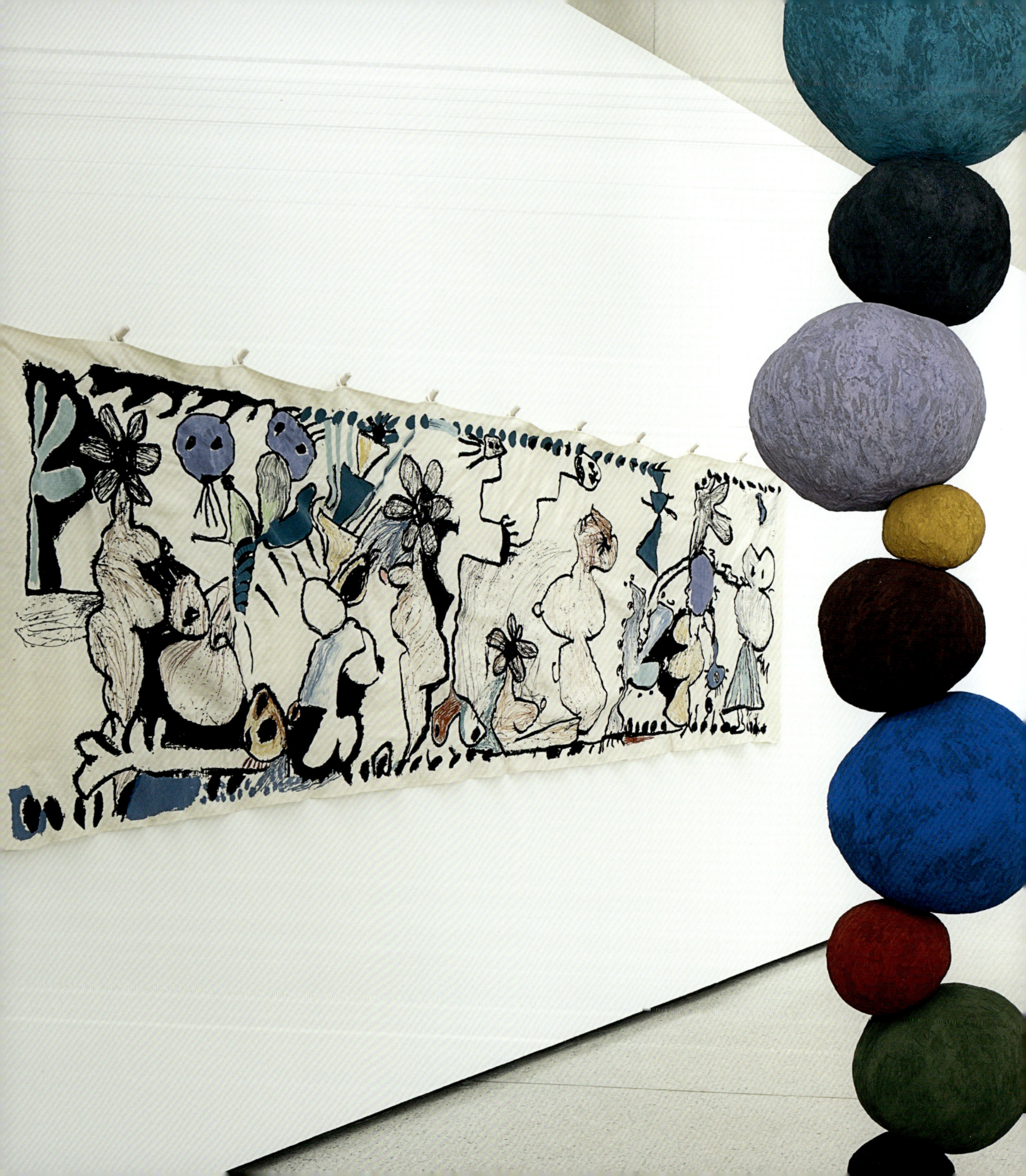

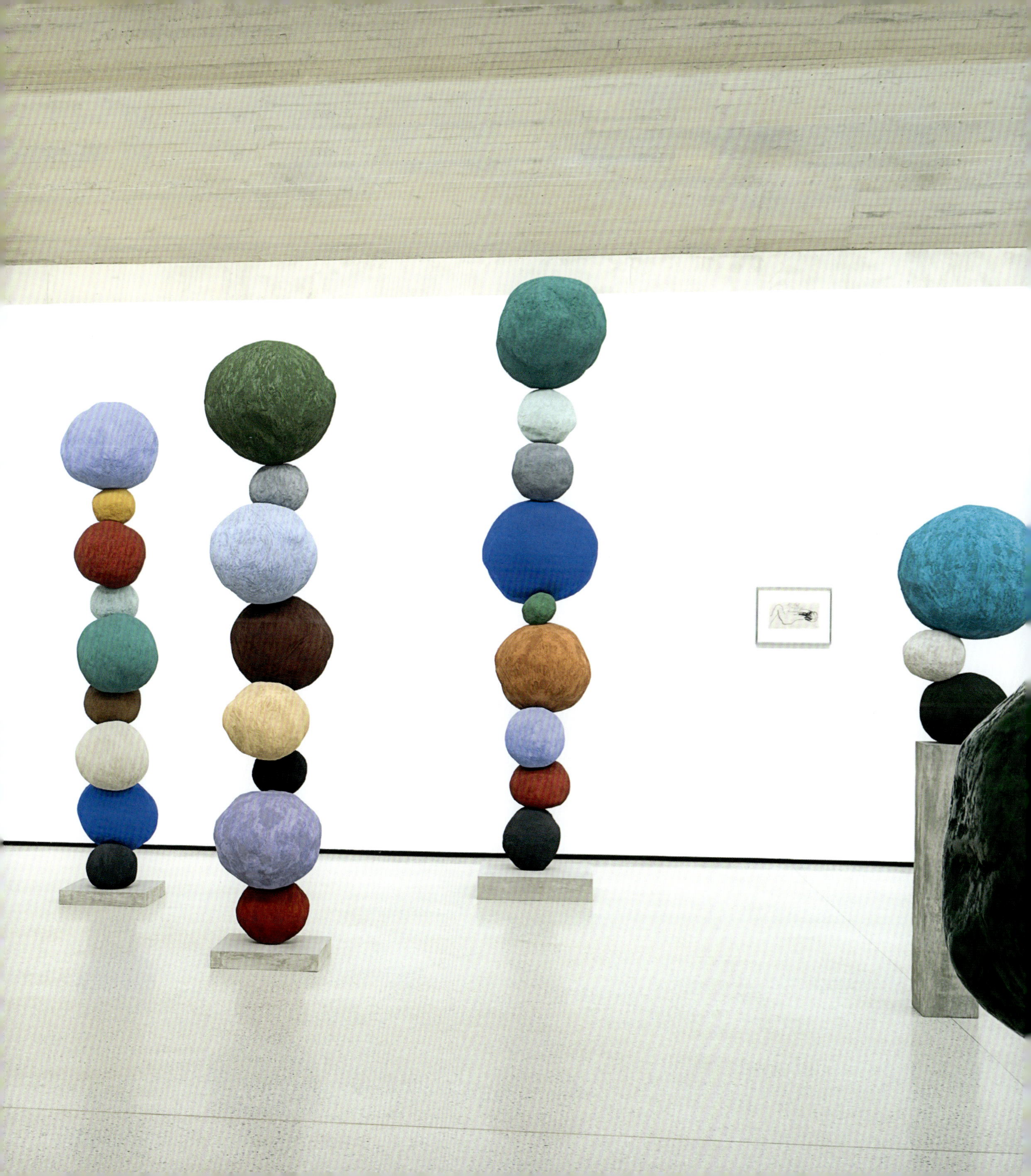

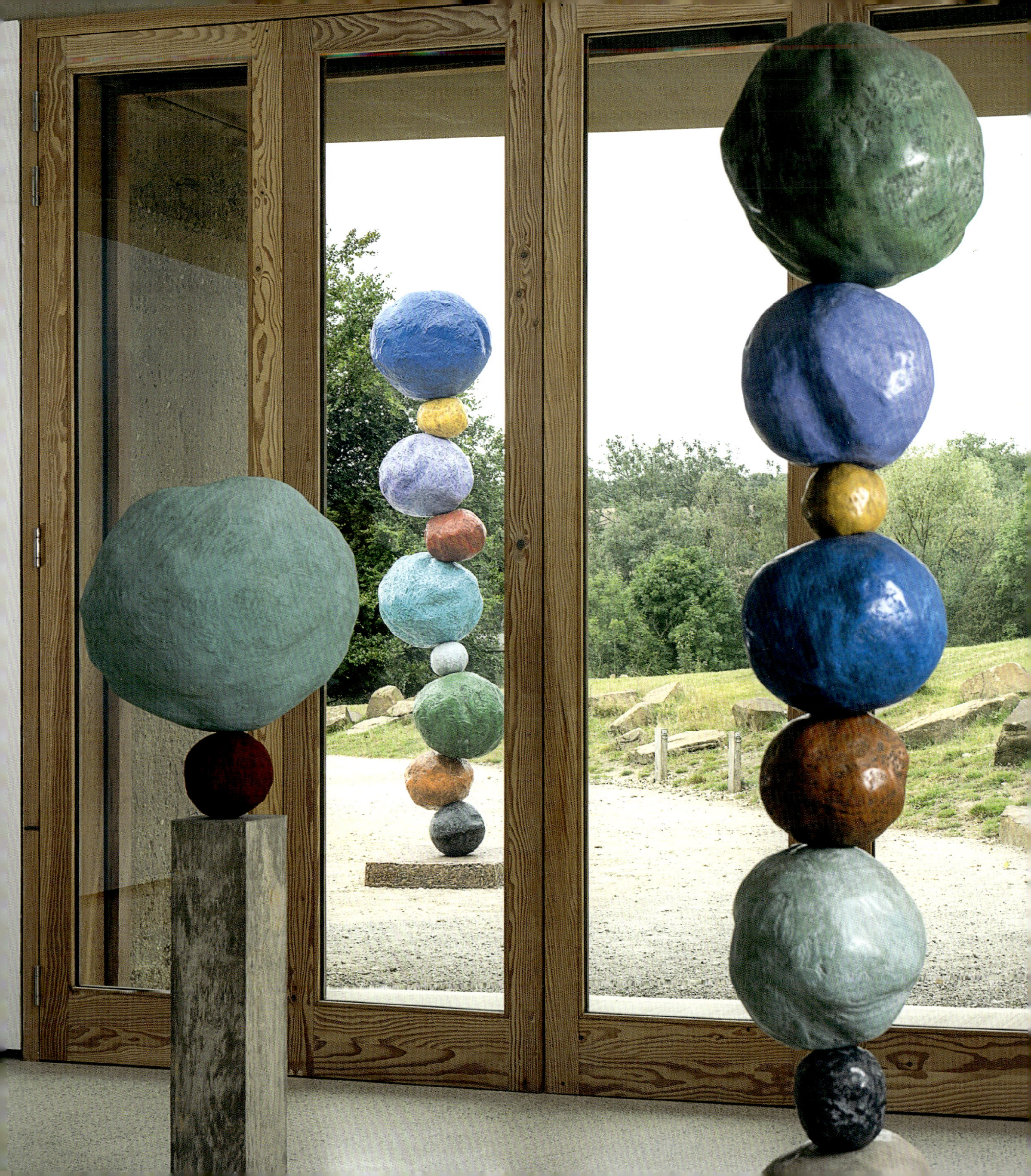

Foldout: *Night Landscape* 2021, thread on cotton. Photograph Jonty Wilde

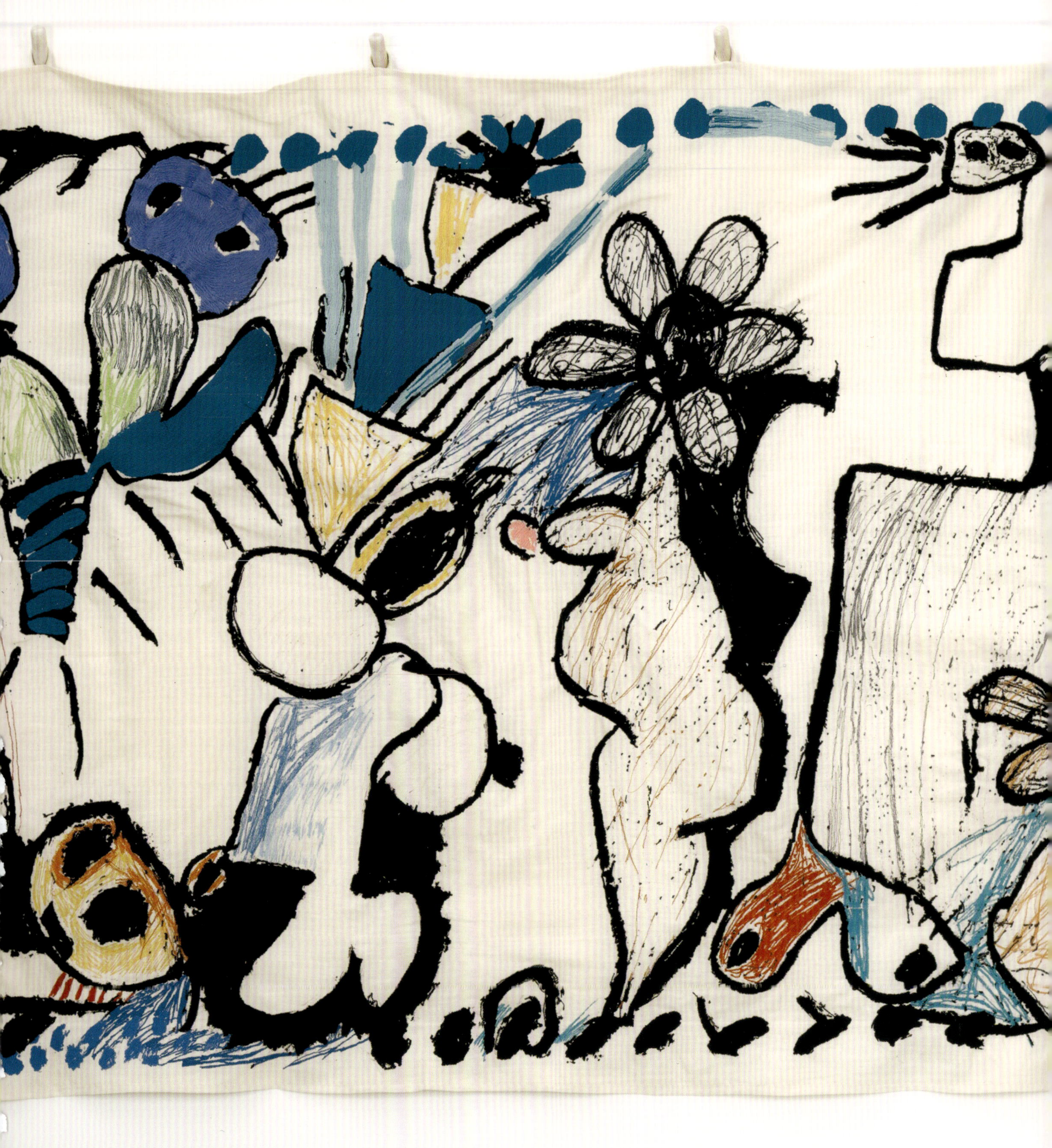

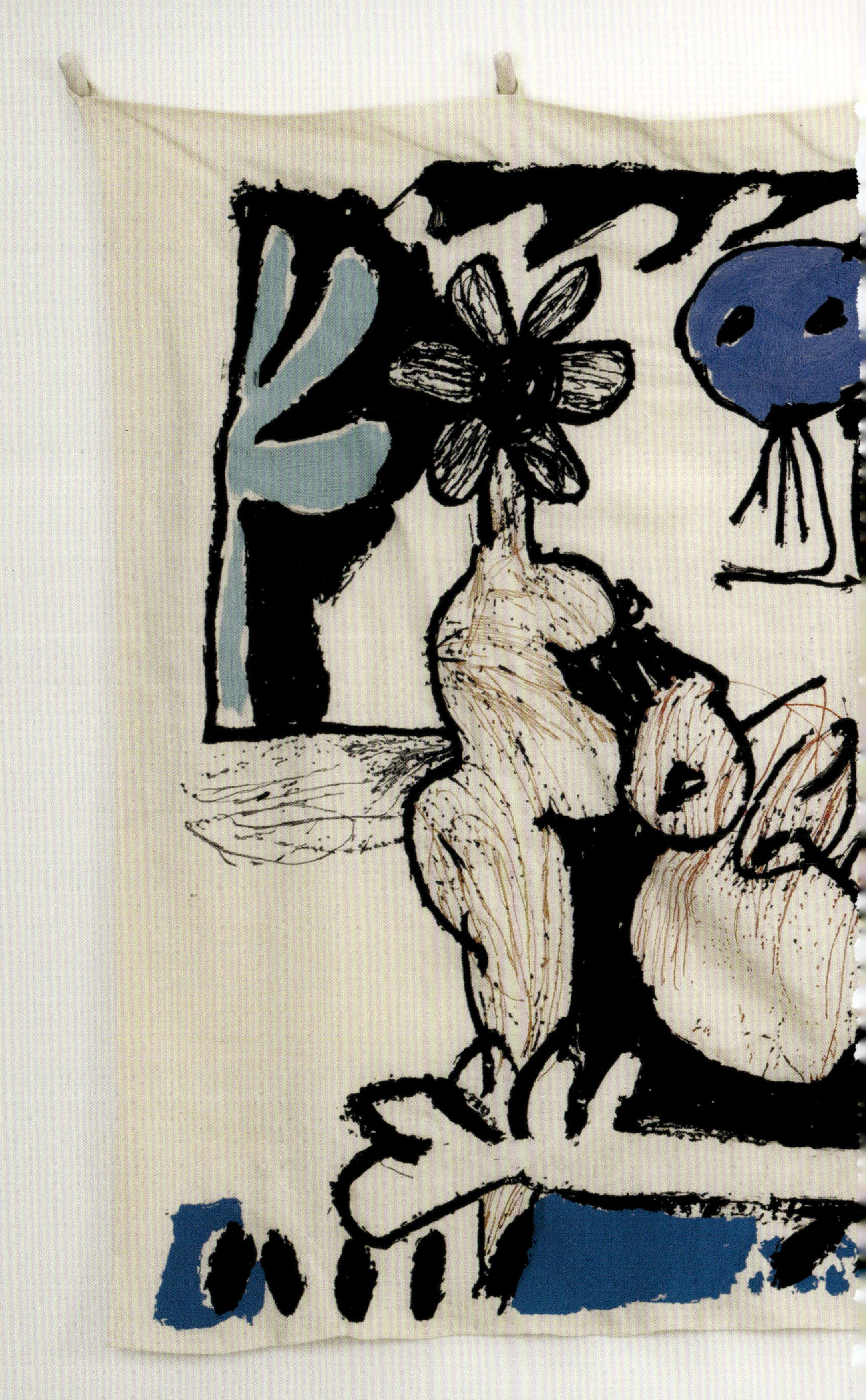

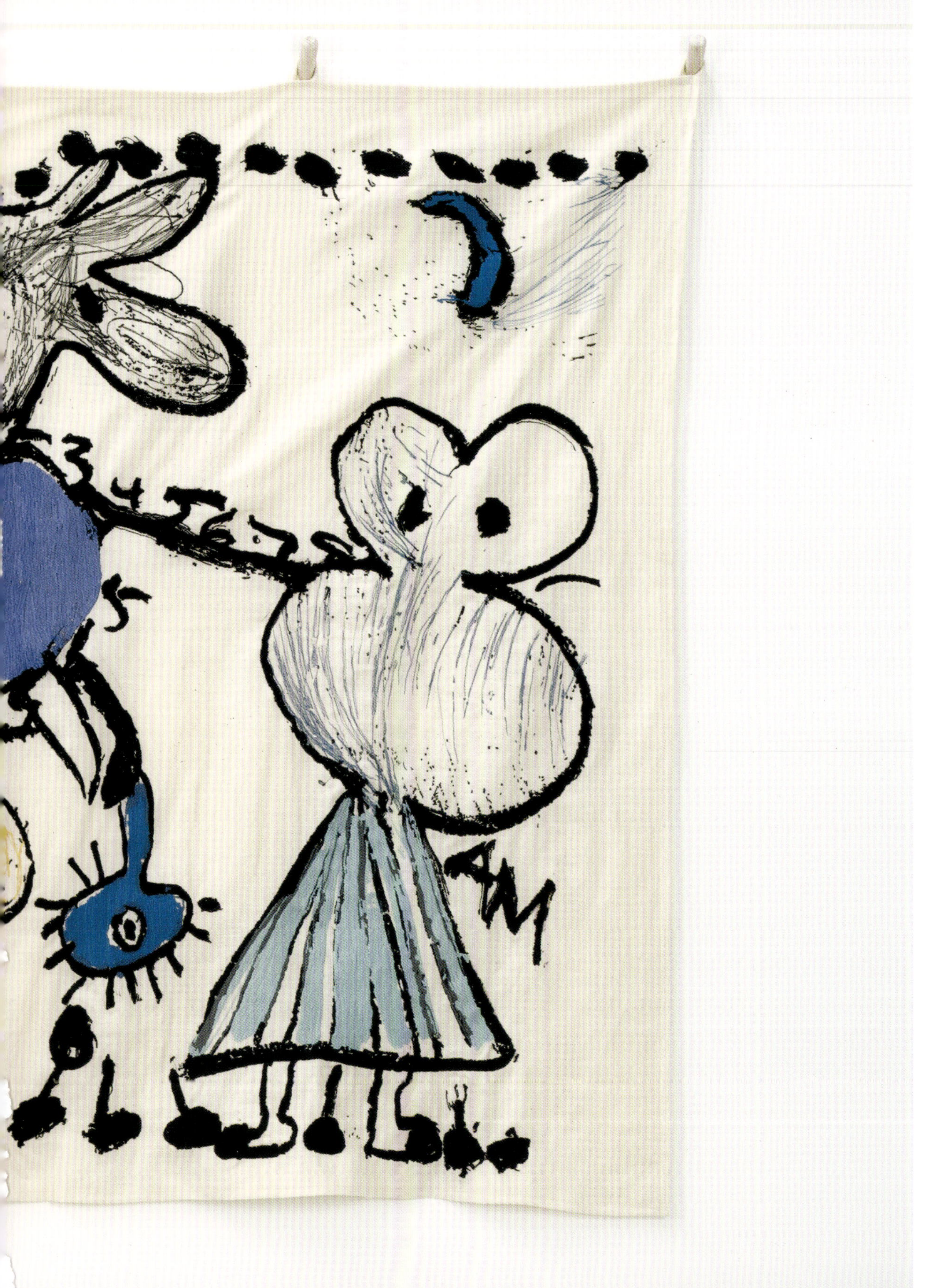

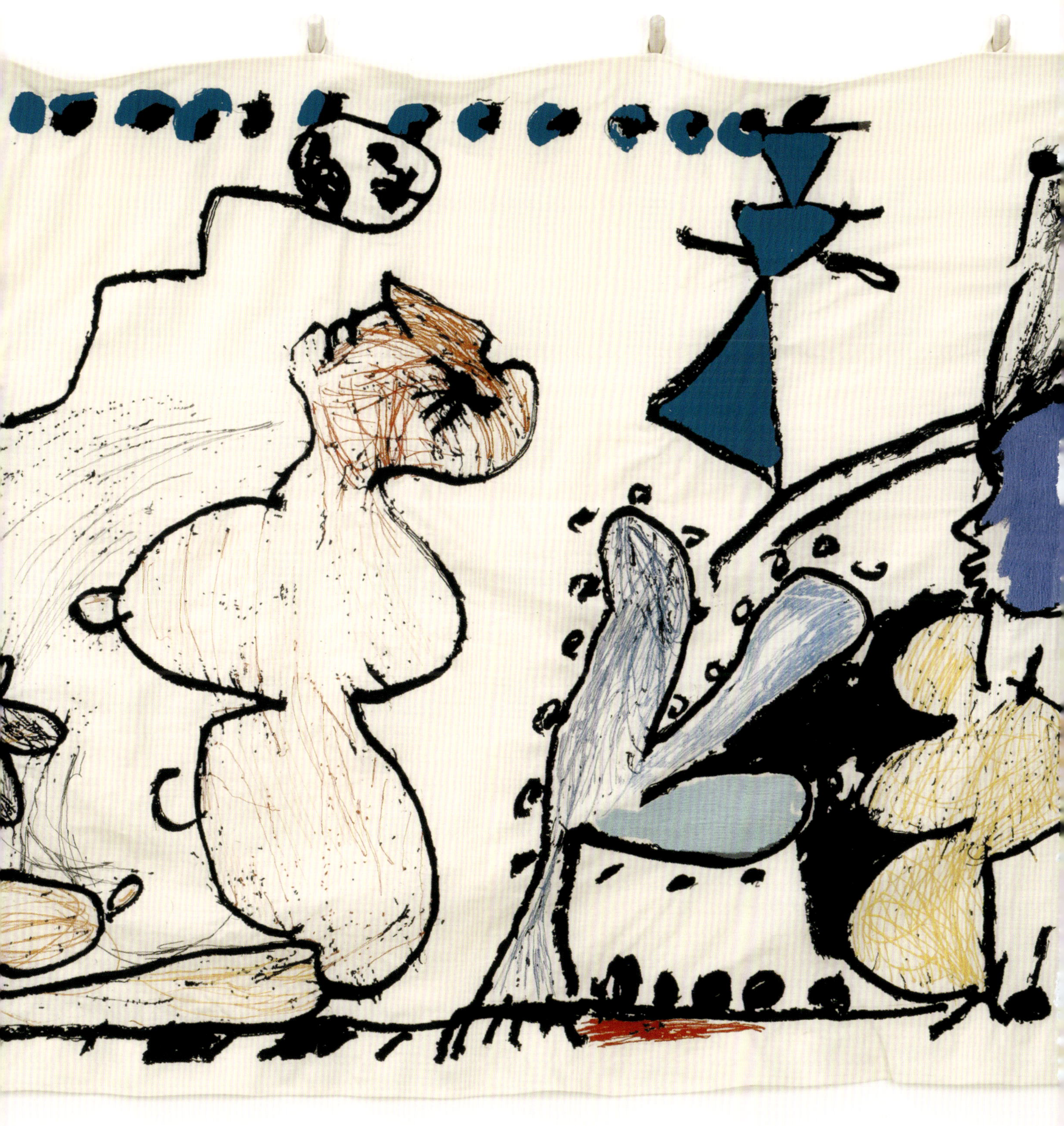

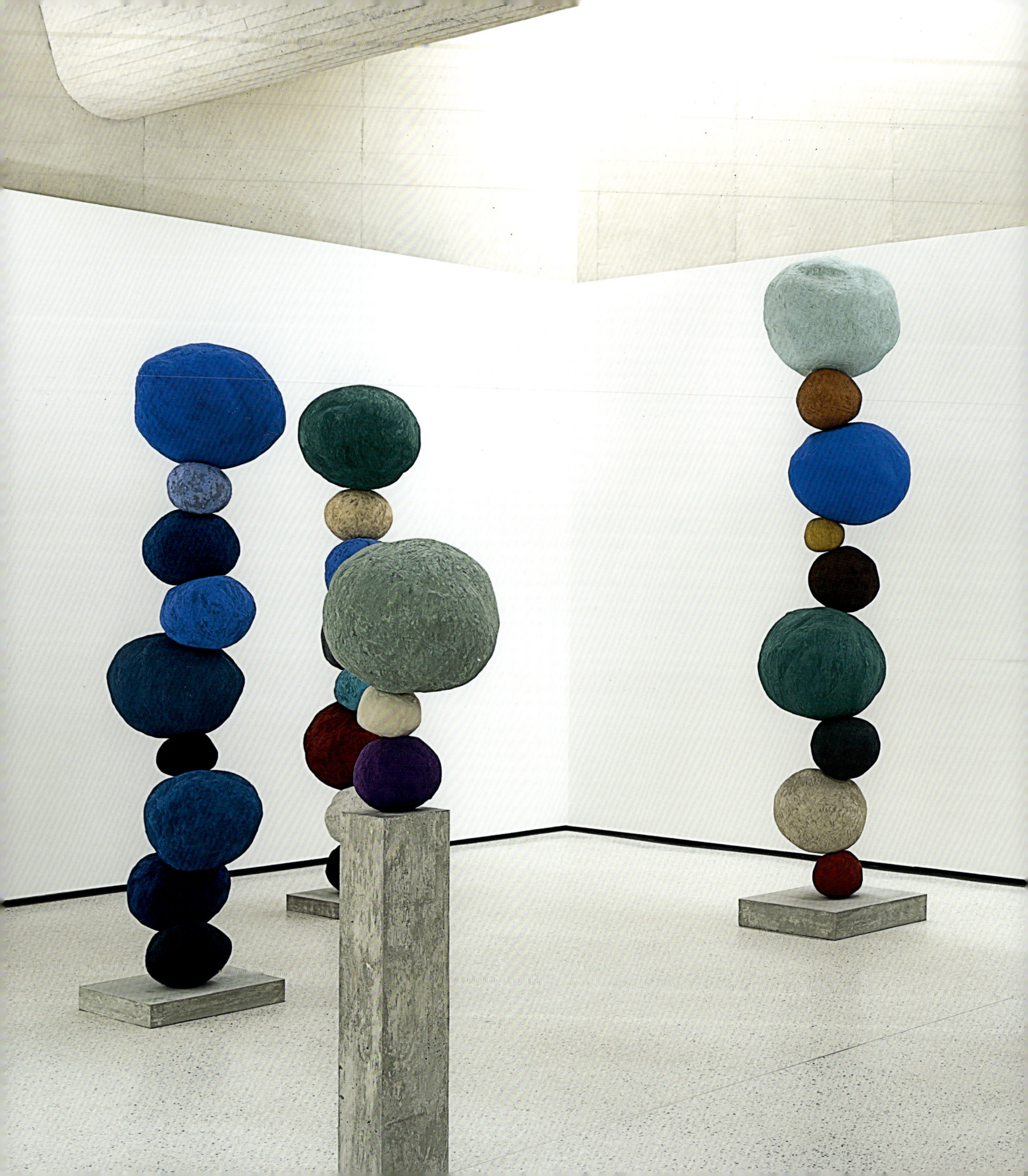

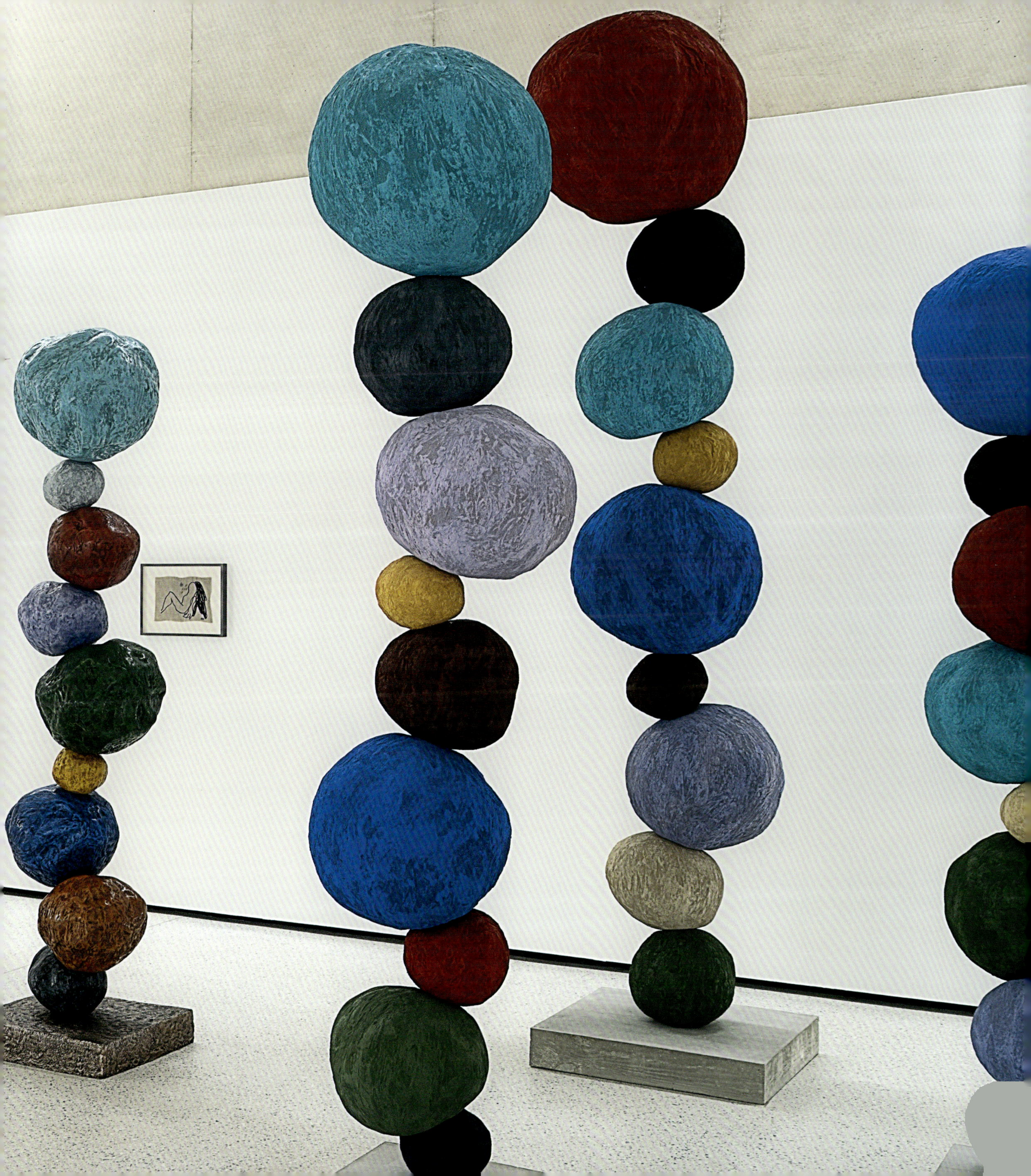

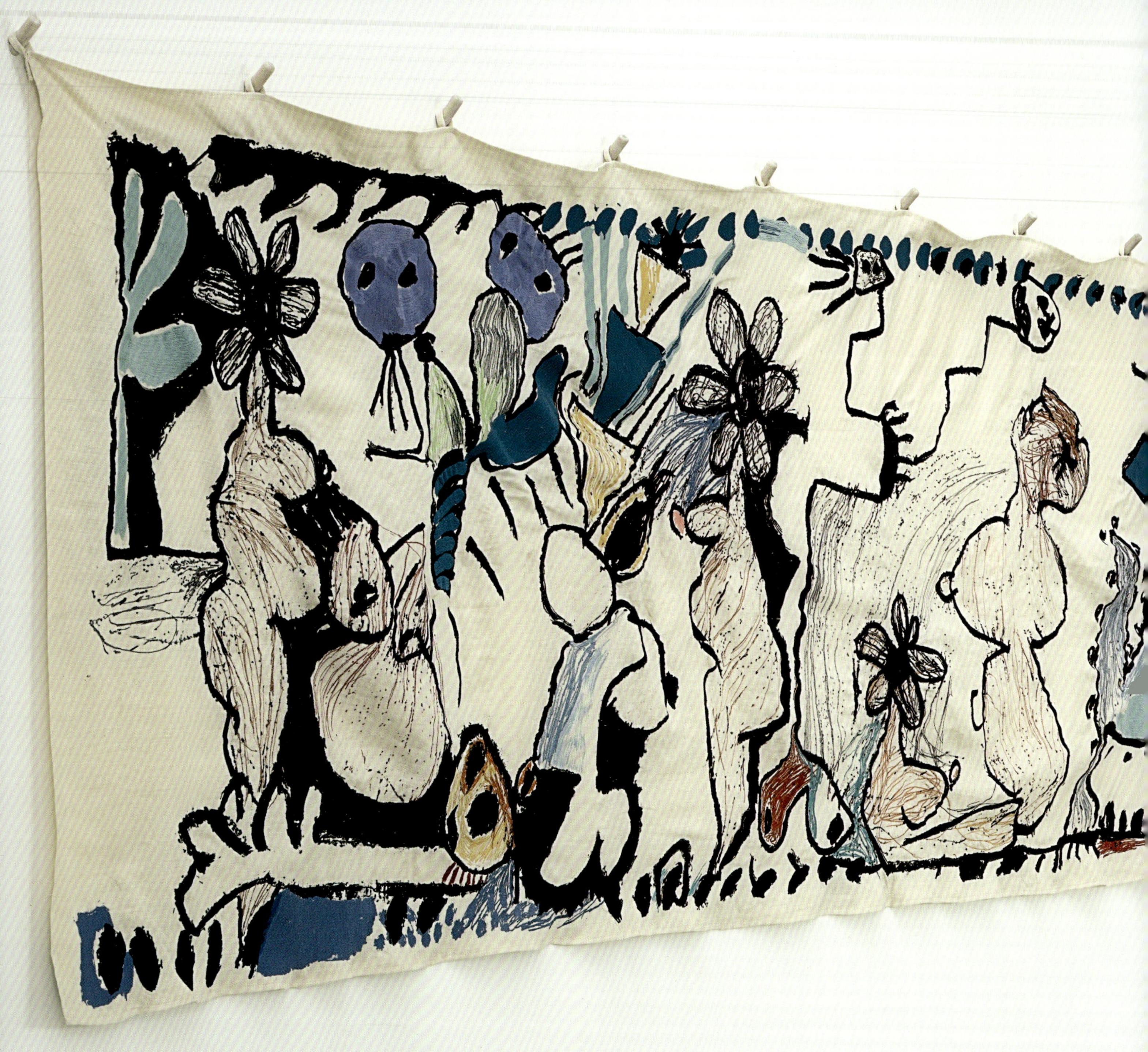

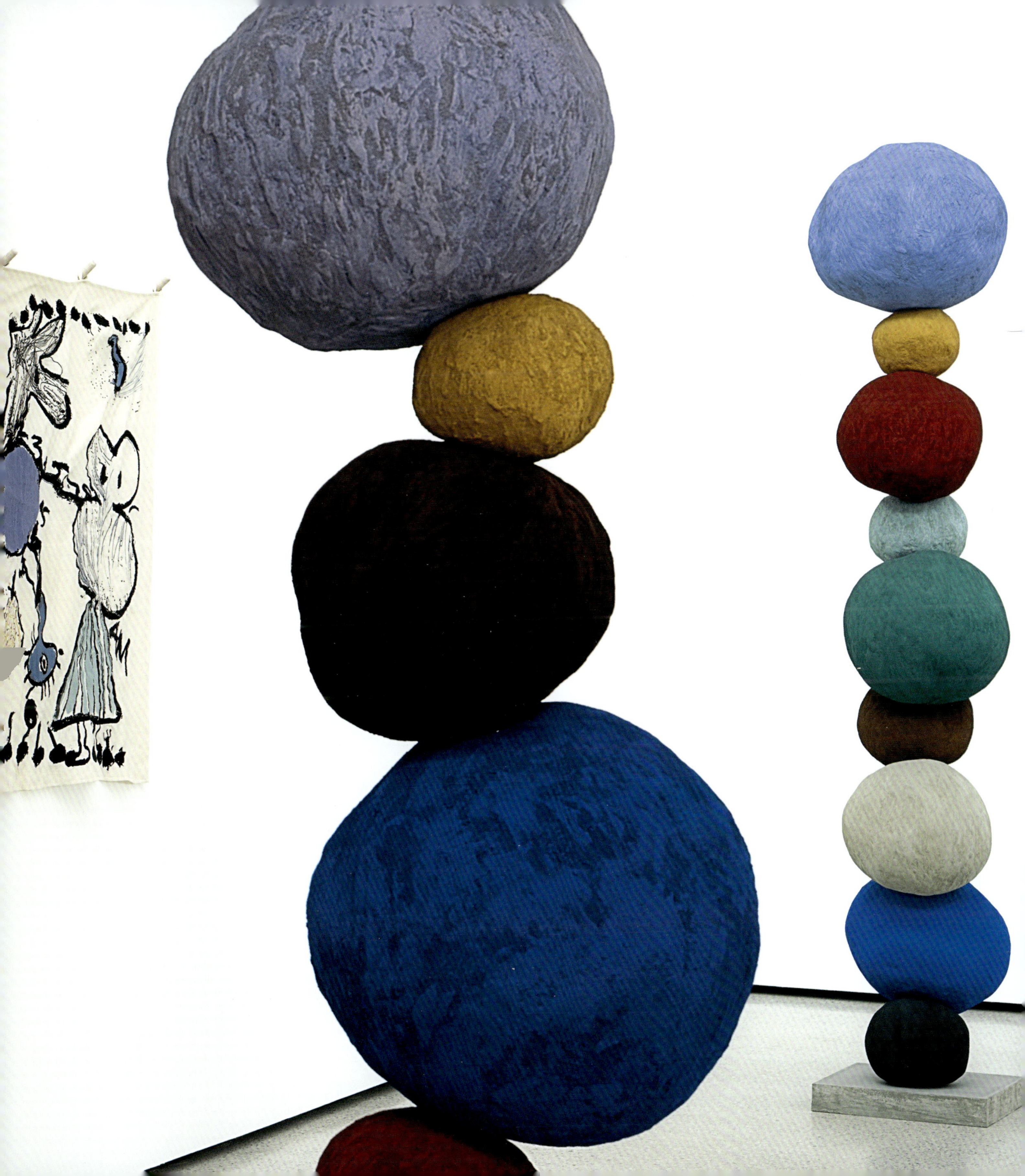

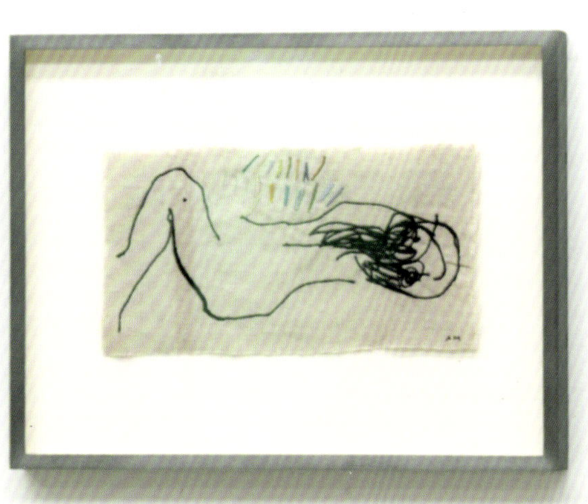

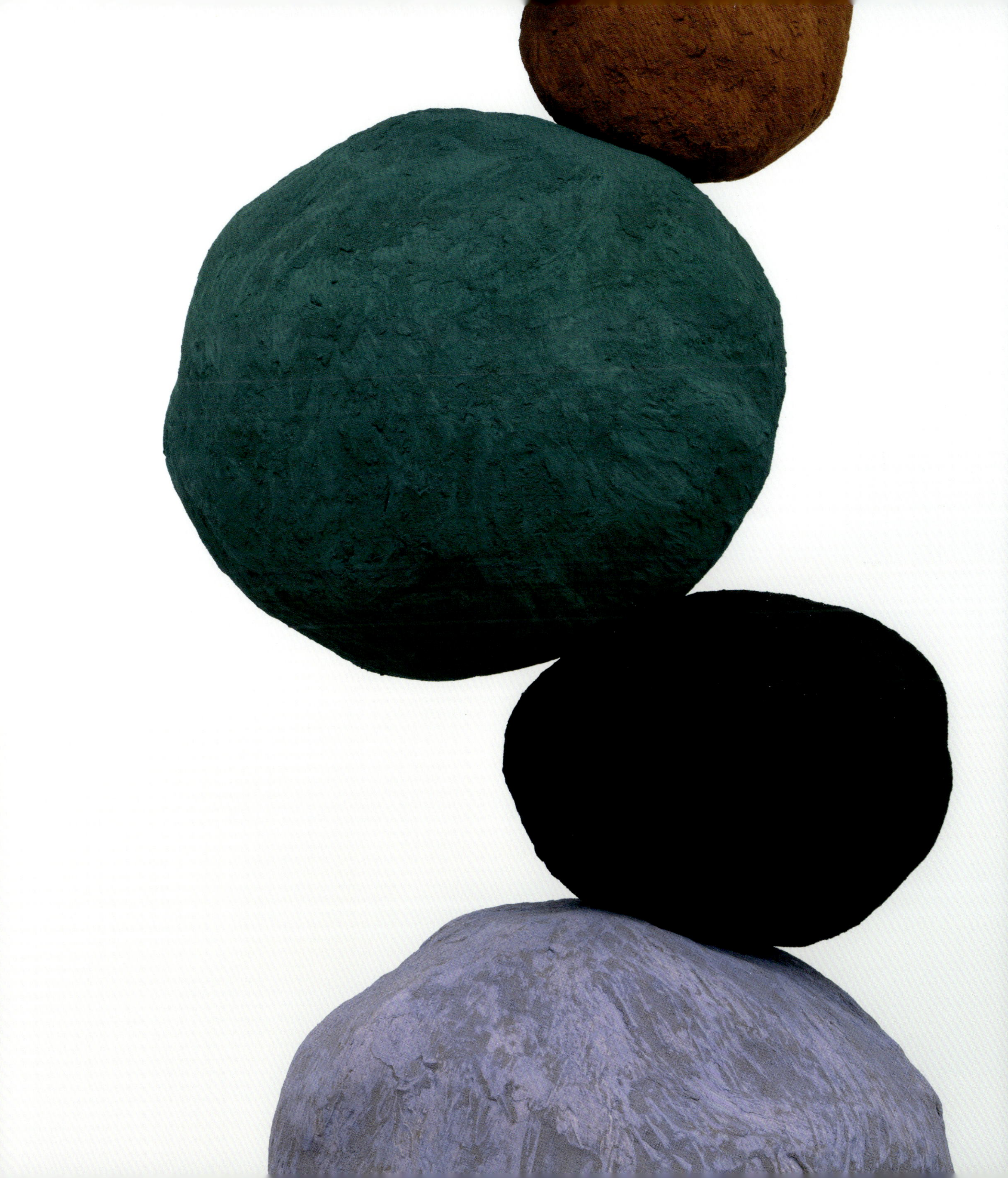

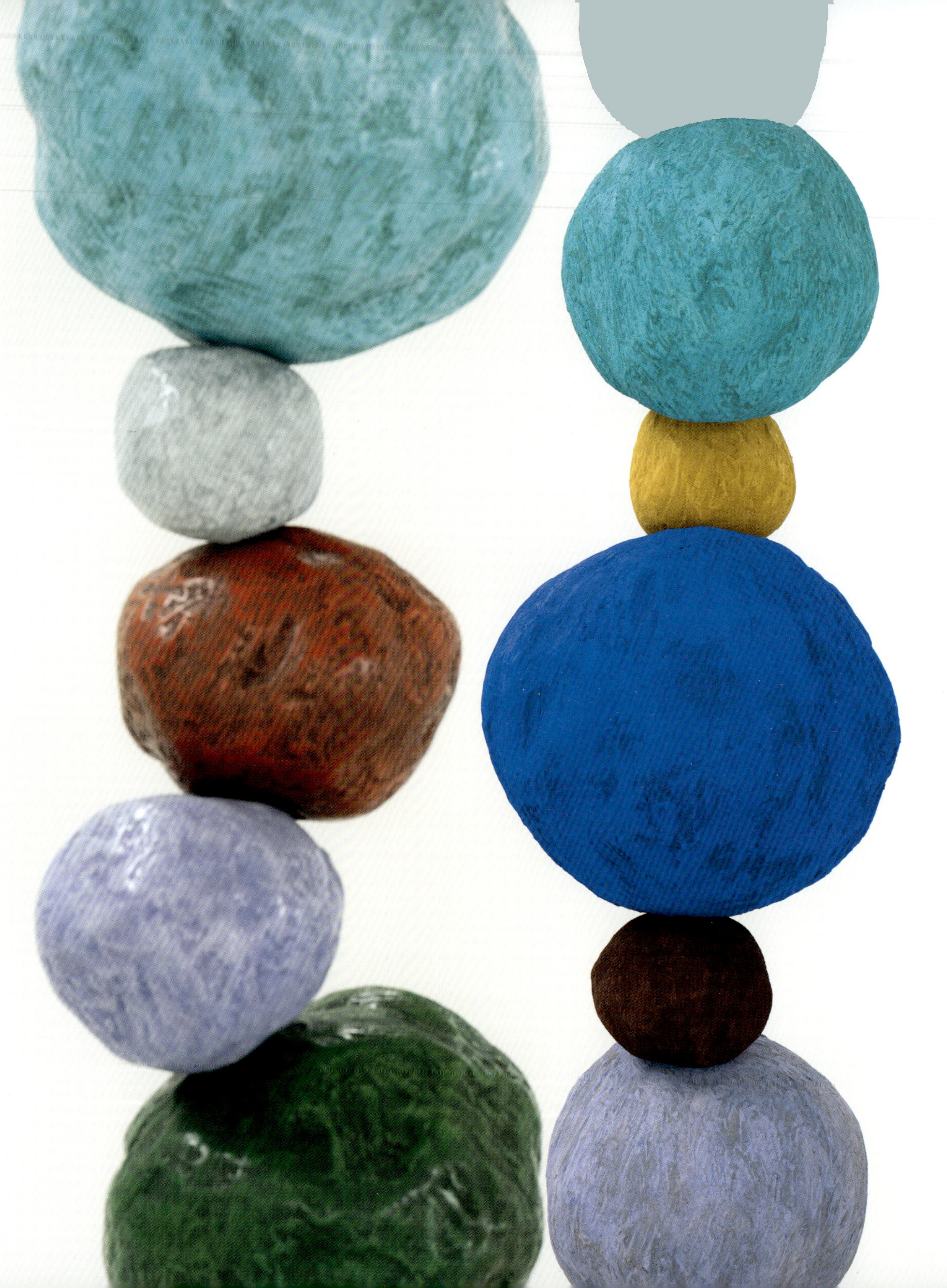

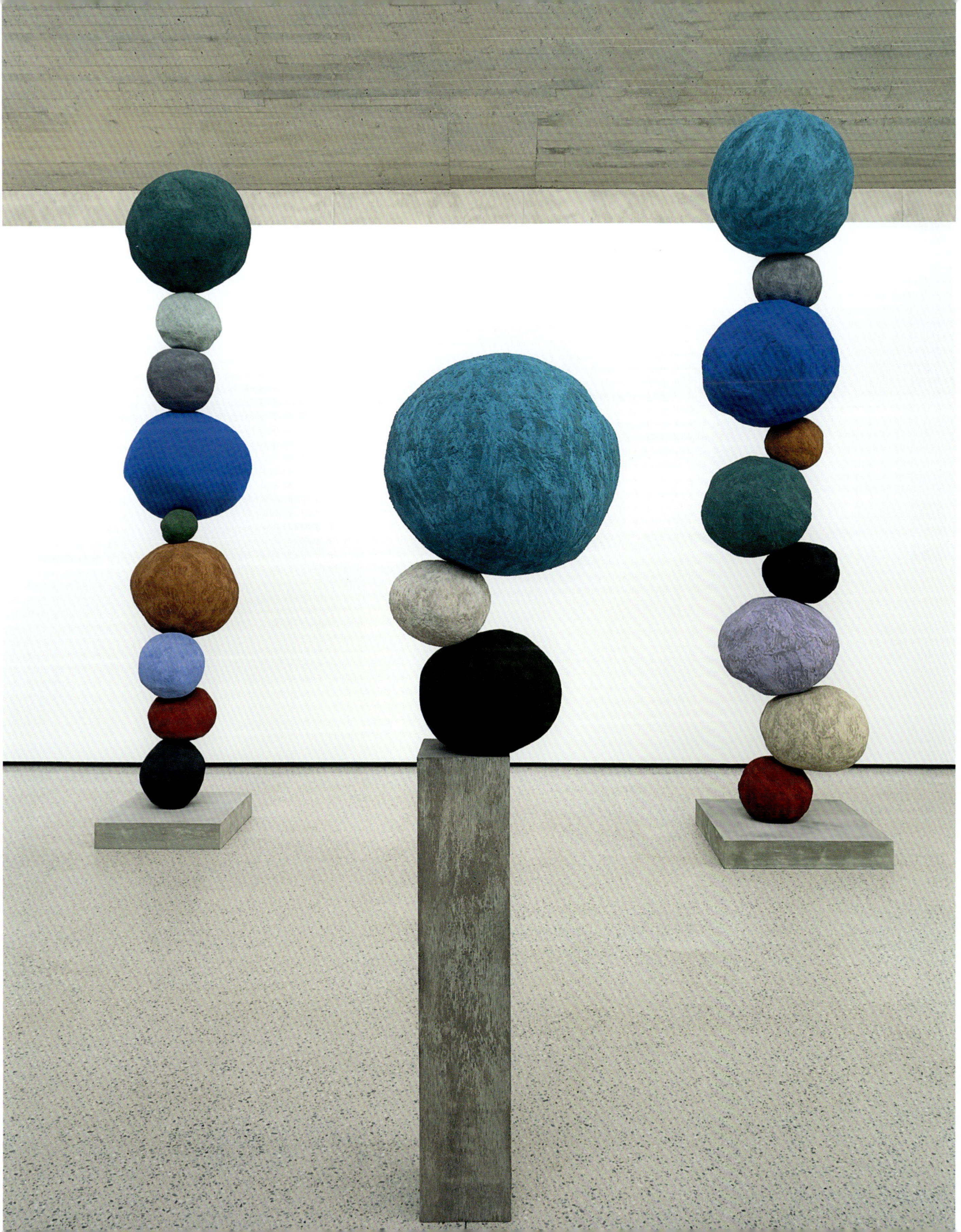

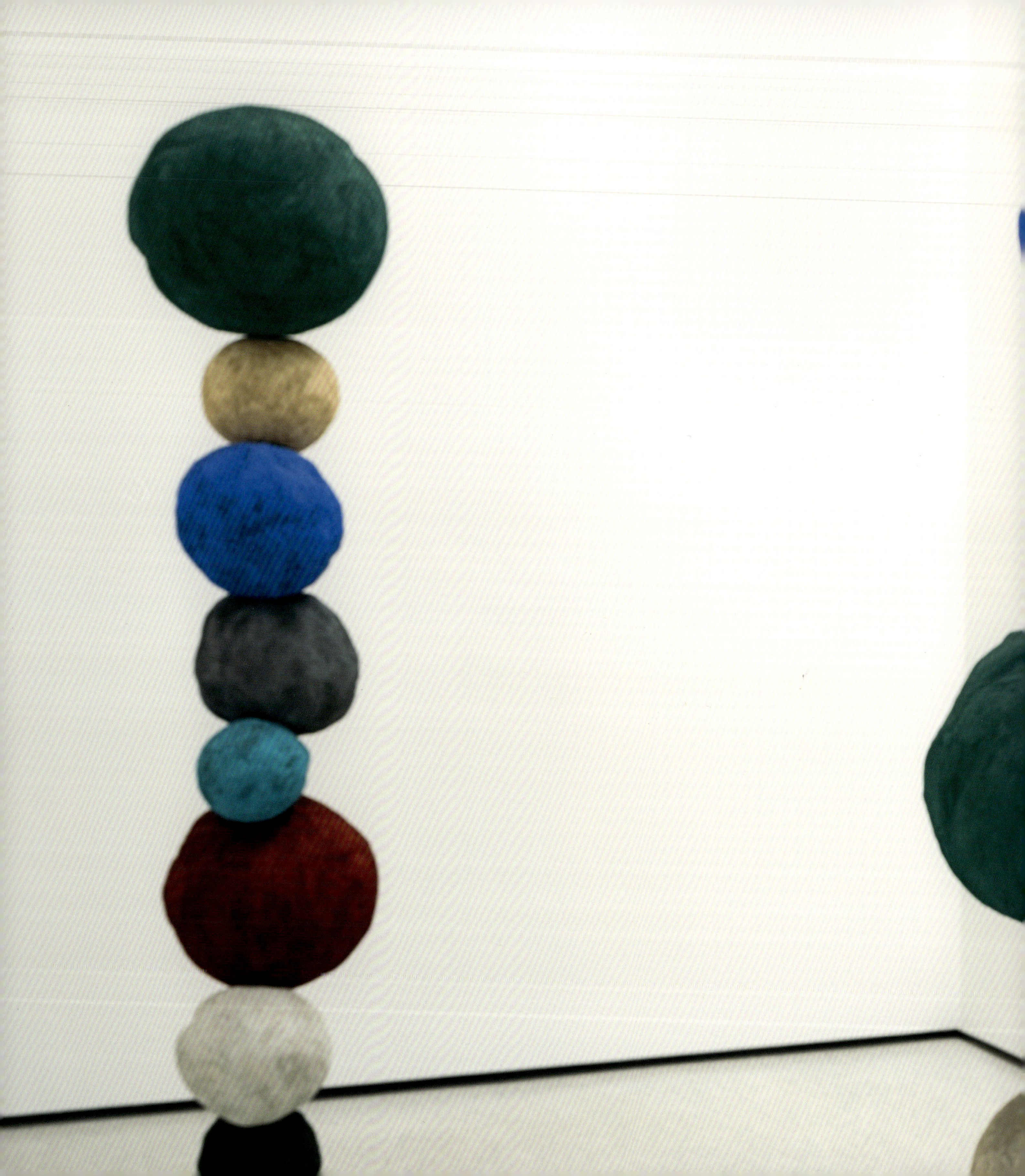

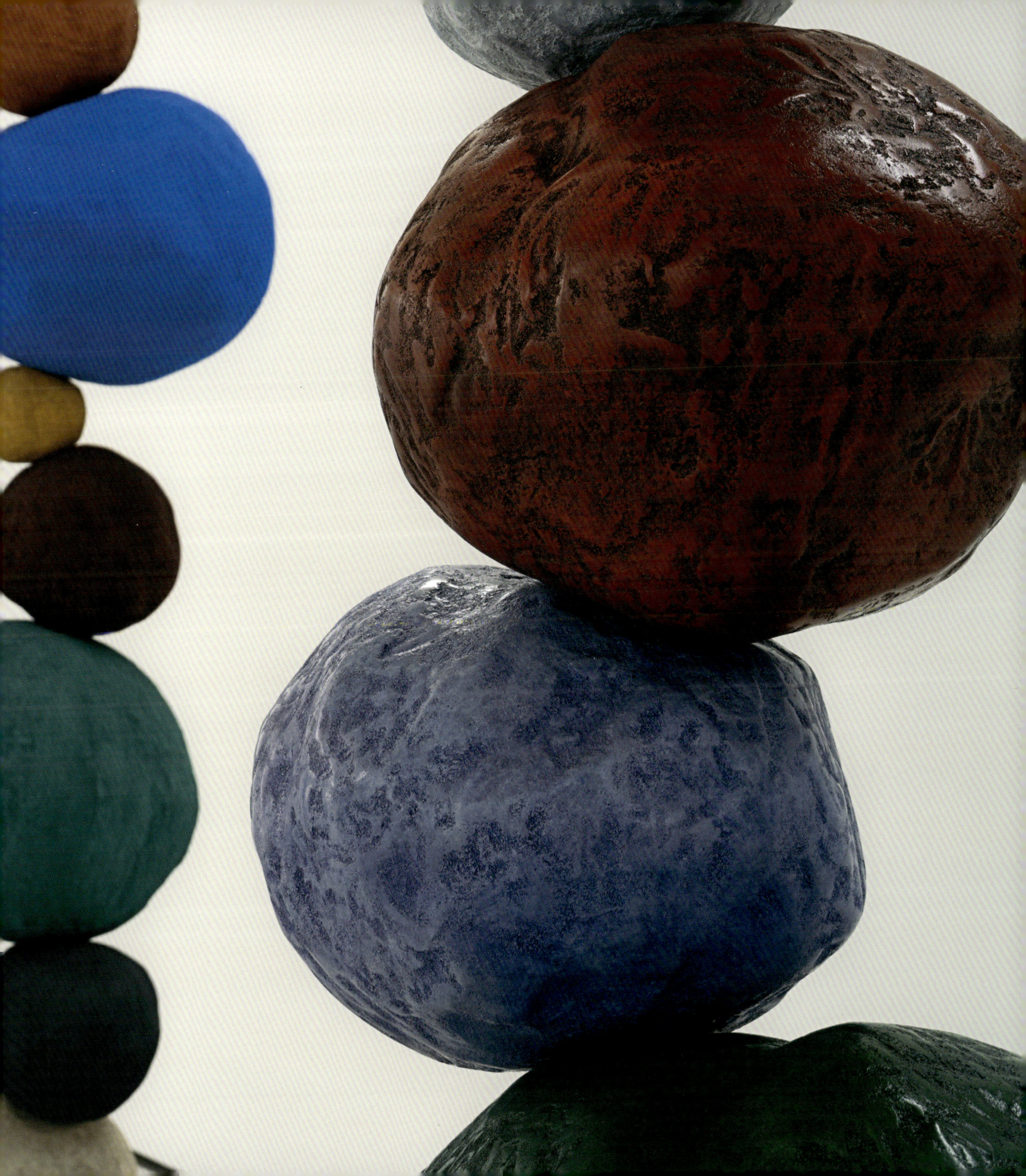

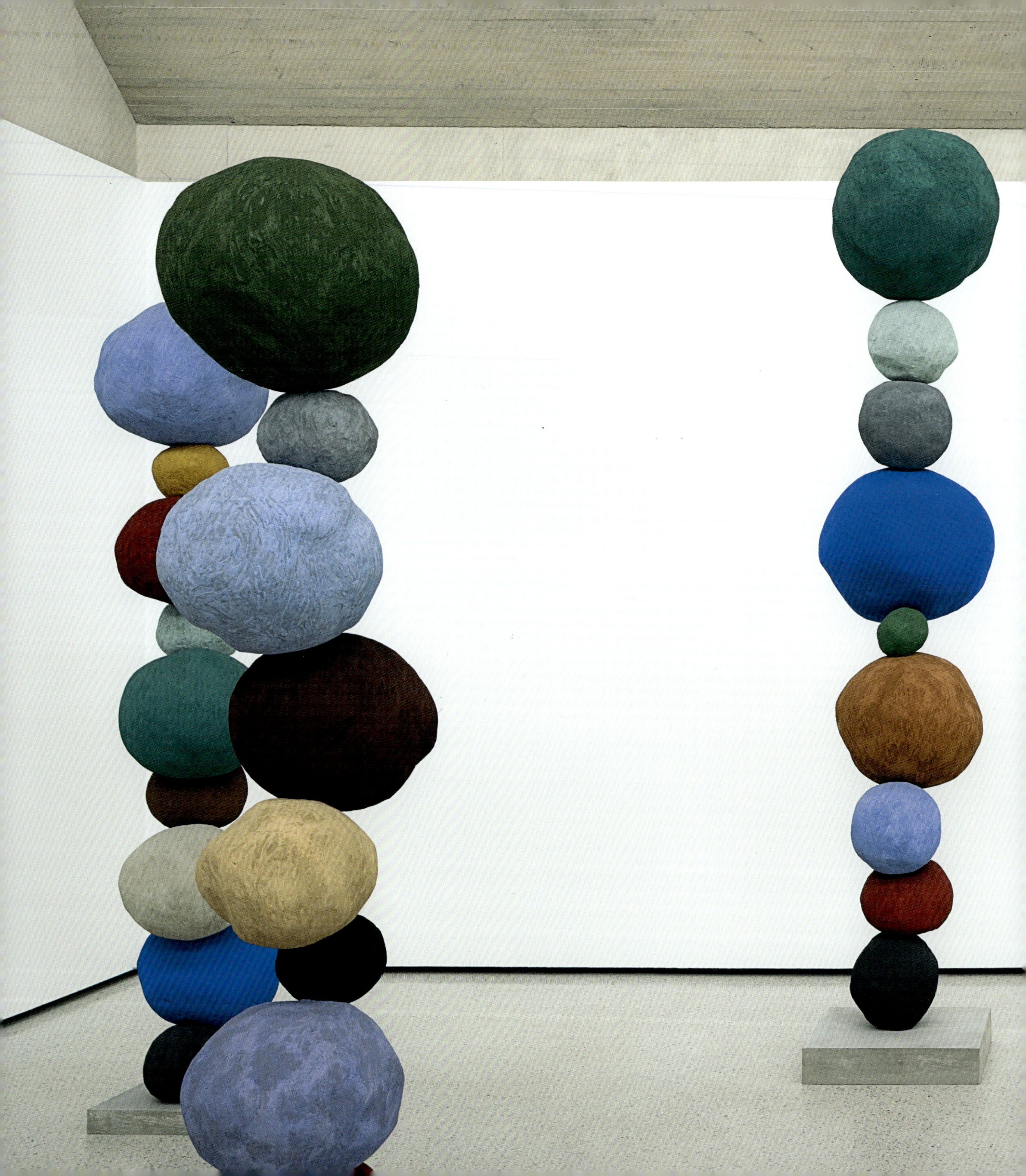

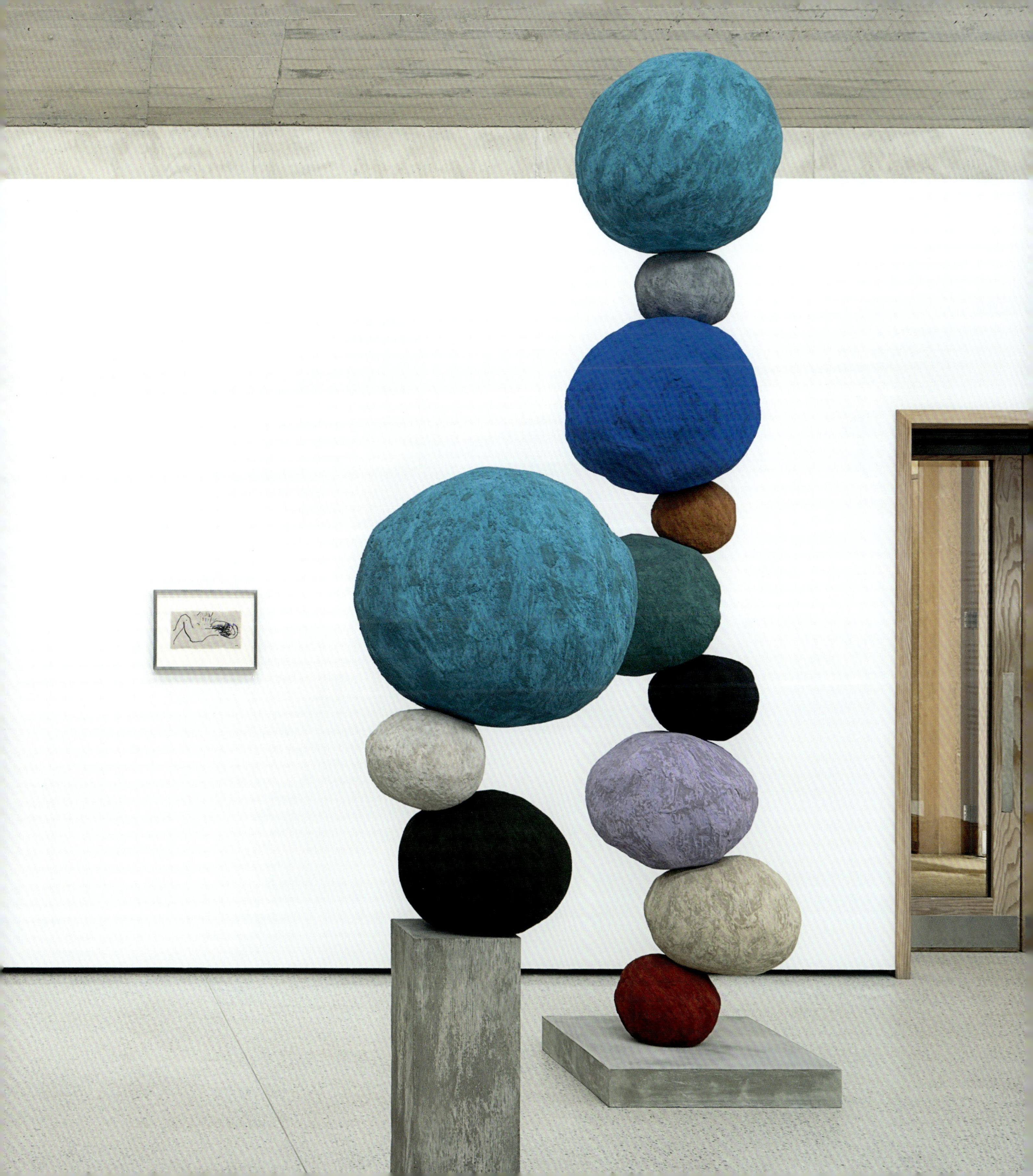

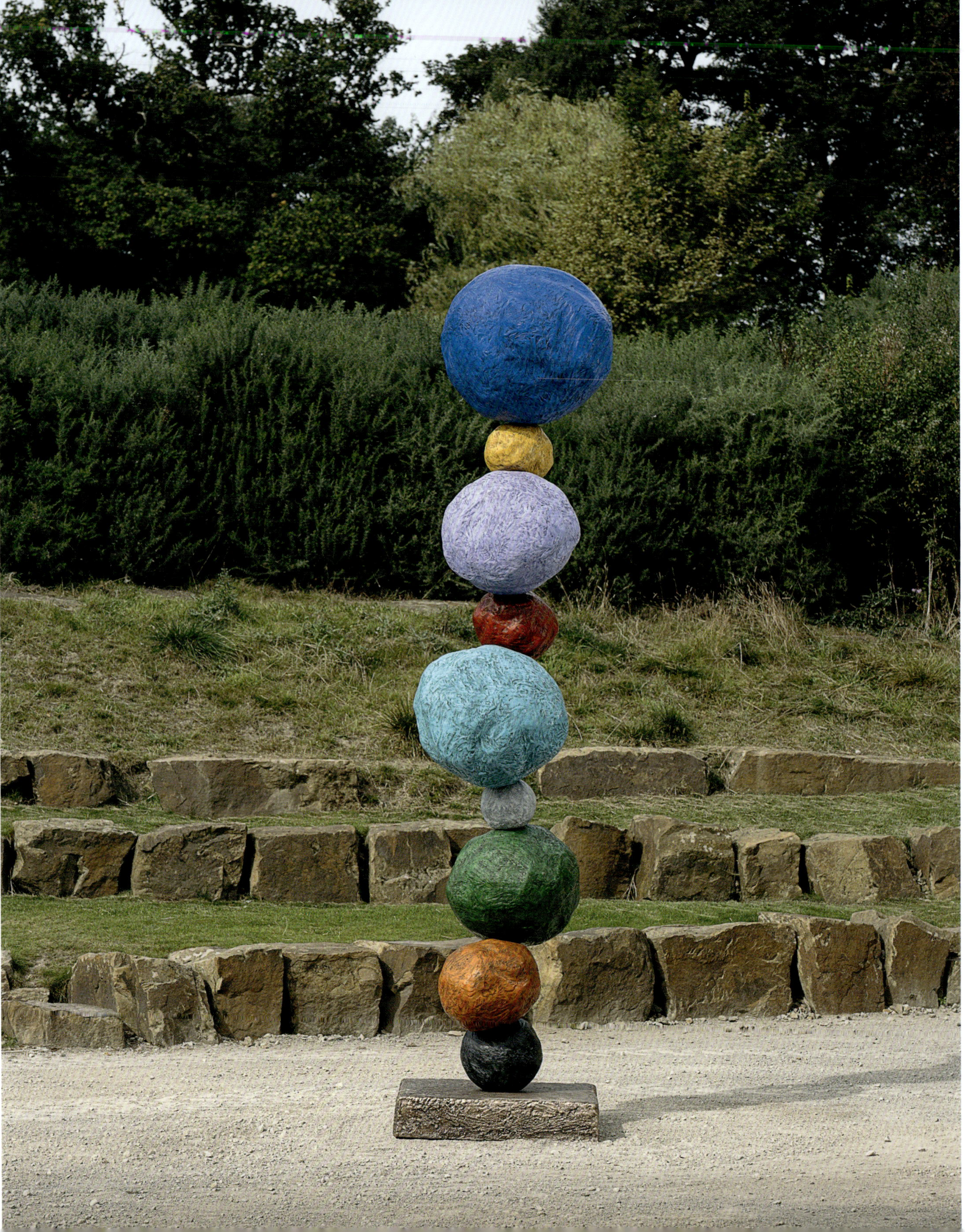

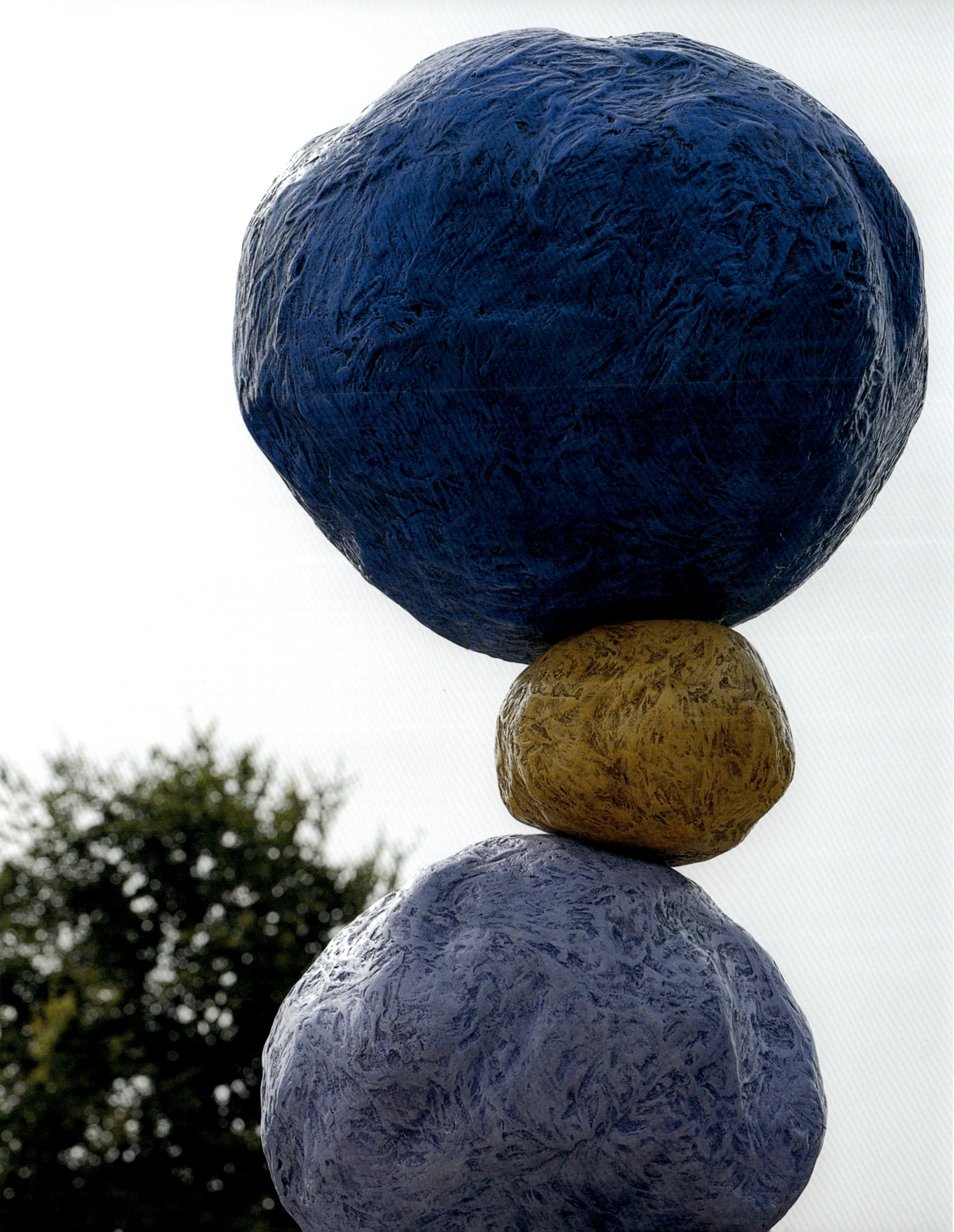

INTERVIEW WITH DAVID TRIGG

Originally published in the online journal *Studio International*

David Trigg: Your most recognisable body of work is your *Stack* series, begun in 2014 and inspired by a personal tragedy. How important is it to you that the viewer knows the backstory of this continuing series?

Annie Morris: It's not important, you don't need to know it. In fact, it wasn't known until I mentioned it in an interview once. Looking at the works, you'd never arrive at that conclusion – that I'd made them because of that tragedy and the grief I was going through. The feedback I often get when people talk to me about these works is that they feel very joyous, which to me is exciting.

DT: How then do you feel about the backstory becoming public knowledge?

AM: I'm fine with it because stillbirth is an important subject and I love the idea of using my tragedy to help other people. It is something that happens a lot: about one in every 200 births in England. At the time I didn't know anything about it, that it could happen to someone at that stage of pregnancy, at full term. I was naive. Everybody experiences tragedy at some point in their life and for me these *Stack* pieces are all about what happens afterwards. They have a hopeful quality to them I think, that's what I want them to have.

DT: What prompted you to channel that personal tragedy into your sculptures?

AM: I didn't do therapy or any of the things that you probably should do when you have a shock to your system like that. What really helped me was being able to lose myself in drawing. I spent time in the studio making these very obsessive ballpoint pen drawings; they were large and had these random balls in them, and faceless women – they were all about what I'd gone through with losing the baby. They were sad drawings because it was just such a dark time for me. Then I began introducing some little coloured lines, which were like the beginning of hope. For me, colour has always been something very hopeful and joyous, it's what I turn to when I feel sad and, on a simple level, it just makes me feel happy. Those coloured lines were the starting point for the sculptures because I realised that they were what I wanted to focus on.

I wanted to get away from the negativity. It then felt very natural to use the ball shape that I had been drawing because it was obviously the shape that had gone, the shape that I'd lost. I didn't think I was going to get pregnant again and this shape was very comforting.

DT: Some people would want to run away from that reminder.

AM: That's a good point but for me it was – and still is – comforting to make this work because in a small way it keeps that thing alive, that thing that I wanted so much, which was taken away. As time went on I became more interested in balance and in exaggerated shapes and forms. I love the way that in these sculptures the larger balls teeter on the smaller balls in a defiance of gravity. I like that they seem impossible.

DT: What comes first, the colours or the arrangement of the balls?

AM: I work out the form first so that the balance is right. I tend to mock it up in watercolour. I make the balls in another studio, which is really messy. I carve them from hardened foam, a very simple material, which is then covered in layers of sand and plaster. I want the works to look raw and immediate so the carving is quite crude, and they keep changing shape as I go. Then I'll bring them to my painting studio where I apply the pigment. If it doesn't feel right I'll replaster, re-sand and then repaint, so there's a lot of moving and changing of colour when I work on them. I have a lot of different elements on the go at once. I've investigated and trialled so many ways of doing it and I've got to know the way in which pigment reacts to different materials. For me it's really all about the surface; I'm really fascinated with the surface and textures of paintings, and I want to make it look as if the paint hasn't dried on these sculptures. I love the vividness of raw pigment and I'm desperately trying to preserve that intensity. My earlier stacks aren't as vibrant but now I know how these pigments behave, so if I'm using an ultramarine blue, I know how to layer it so that it does what I want.

DT: I have seen them described as totems, is that something you are happy with?

AM: I don't mind how people describe them but I don't call them that. I call them stacks, which is useful for naming and cataloguing but really for me they are just paintings, a sort of three-dimensional sculptural painting.

DT: You regularly use vivid ultramarine blue, viridian green and yellow ochre pigments in your sculptures. What informs your colour choices?

AM: My colour selection is intuitive but quite specific now because I've got to know these colours so well. I'm always searching for new colours though; I do a lot of oil-stick drawing so I often just play around with different colours. I'm using a new colour this year that I call *Rome White* because I discovered it when I was doing a show in Rome; it's a hazy, not-quite-white but not-quite-buff titanium that has a beautiful softness to it. I also get a lot of inspiration from just walking around: I may see a blue car passing a red one and love the combination, or find colours I like in other artists' paintings. I'm mixing a lot of the colours in the studio now, which is a new development. Slight differences create real excitement for me. There's a new light ultramarine that I've recently started using that's really exciting but it's very difficult to use because it's an extremely strong colour; as soon as you use it there's a need for balance because I don't like it when one colour jumps out. I really love putting it with a purple pigment called caput mortuum.

DT: Have you explored different configurations of the balls other than stacking?

AM: No, I'm not interested because I find the stacks very comforting. I like the forms I'm working with and I'm not ready to move on to something else. Having said that, I have been thinking about maybe making some hanging sculptures. But I've been thinking more about scale. Next year I'm making a giant 5.5-metre (18ft) bronze for a show at Château La Coste in Provence. Working on that scale is very exciting. I've also made a huge stack sculpture with three balls for my show at Timothy Taylor, it's the largest one I've ever made and I've got to complete it in the gallery because it's too big to fit through the door. I'm also going to be pairing my new two and three ball sculptures as I like the conversations that happen between them. In that way they've become slightly more figurative.

DT: You've also made a 3.5-metre-tall bronze stack for your exhibition at Yorkshire Sculpture Park.

AM: That was difficult because I've never made anything on that scale before. I initially carved it in my studio because I wanted a 1:1 model, to see the size. Everyone said I was insane because I could have just made a small maquette. I had originally intended to make the piece 5.5 metres tall but there were so many covid-related problems that it didn't happen. Bronze is really exciting and I worked with Pangolin Editions to create the sculpture at its amazing foundry. At YSP I'm showing it just outside the Weston Gallery. Inside, I'm showing several large stacks. I want the show to feel like you're walking into my studio – I keep a lot of work in my studio and there's always a forest of sculptures, so I wanted to replicate the impact of seeing all those works together in one space.

DT: YSP is a great location to show a forest of bronzes.

AM: I admire Barbara Hepworth's *The Family of Man* (1970), on long-term loan and display at YSP. It's such an interesting and beautiful work. If there was a way, one day, of creating something similar that comprises several elements coming together as one – a family or forest of bronze works – that would be fantastic. I have lots of ideas for public artworks.

DT: Tell me about the title of the exhibition, *When a Happy Thing Falls*.

AM: It comes from a poem by Rainer Maria Rilke, from his *Duino Elegies*. It was a title I originally used for a 2009 drawing. That line just moved me. It's got an ambiguous quality that really resonated with me and I think makes sense for this exhibition. It alludes to the reason for these works and also to this moment we've all been through. I like the idea of a happy thing being embodied as an object, and then thinking about how you respond when it falls and what happens next.

DT: You mentioned that Barbara Hepworth's sculpture *The Family of Man* is a source of admiration to you. Which artists have you learned the most from?

AM: That's so tough to answer! There are certain artworks that I look at a lot, Henri Matisse's *The Piano Lesson* (1916), for example, and also his *Snail* (1953). Artists that I go back to over the years include Willem de Kooning and Robert Rauschenberg – there's a freedom to their works that I love and want for my work too. I would also have to say Louise Bourgeois, the relationship she had with her father resonated with me. I remember reading about that as a young artist and feeling extremely moved. I had the wonderful experience of meeting her at her studio before she died.

DT: Apart from Bourgeois, all of those artists are painters.

AM: I've always been interested in painters, perhaps even more so than sculptors. I'm also interested in people's drawings, there's something about the immediacy of someone's hand on a page that really fascinates me.

DT: Drawing is of course central to your own practice. Your drawing language is very distinctive.

AM: Everything for me stems from drawing. As a kid I used to draw incessantly. For me, drawing is very instinctive. I like placing huge pieces of paper on the floor, sometimes maybe five or six metres long; I move all the furniture from the studio, unroll a long piece, and just draw. I like to work really fast. I'm such an impatient person so I draw as quickly as I can to get from one end of the paper to the other. If I spend too long on a drawing, I get out of the zone of concentration, so I work better if I do something quickly. I use oil-sticks, crayons and even highlighters so that I can vary the line, mixing thick lines with thin ones.

DT: The work you make now has something of a primal, childlike quality to it.

AM: Yes, you're right, my drawings do have a childlike quality. I'm really attracted to children's drawings. After the age of 12 a child's drawings will start to become self conscious but at around the ages of five or six they have an amazing freedom and I want my work to have that freedom too. Someone once said to me that a successful work is a work that a child might like.

DT: You often return to the same motifs. What is their significance?

AM: I often just draw things as they come into my mind, but I do return to the same characters. I have this flower woman, a female figure whose face I've replaced with a flower. The character started as a kind of self-portrait. She's very quick to do so I quite like using her. The flower is not a pretty flower though, it has nothing to do with beauty, it's much darker than that. It came from something that happened in my childhood, which I remembered years later. I also draw a lot of trees and grids, and there are these figures with hats, which remind me of a very gentlemanly gentleman – he is based on a childhood memory of a very decent man

DT: Is a lot your imagery inspired by childhood events and experiences?

AM: Yes. All my work revolves around the different experiences that I've had or situations I've been in, though without being literal or descriptive. A lot is based on things that I'm not comfortable talking about. My parents got divorced when I was a teenager. In fact, my father had a secret family, which was a super shocking event that still triggers a lot of memories for me. I have a big catalogue of imagery in my head that comes from that experience. It's all about relationships and pain, heartbreak, grief, death and also love, a lot about love. I'm becoming more comfortable with what happened, but I don't really talk about it and I'm never going to be standing there with someone in the gallery, explaining it as they're looking at my work. For me, drawing helps to bring closure to things – I know why I had to make a particular drawing, but that has nothing to do with the reason why someone else might like it.

DT: How has the pandemic affected your practice?

AM: So many things fell through for me. The YSP show was pushed back and my first exhibition in Tokyo was cancelled along with a number of international group shows. I travel so much for work and all that stopped. I moved to the countryside with my family and because I couldn't make my sculptures I did a huge amount of drawing. I was with my children all day so I stayed up really late making drawings, which I loved. I'm quite a late night person anyway, so I liked working at 2am because I didn't have to get up to take the kids to school the next morning. It was a good time to make different work and change things up.

DT: How did your work change during that time?

AM: During the pandemic I was making oil-stick drawings and then sewing over them, trying to make the sewn line look like pen or oil stick. I've been working with sewing for a while, making these quite scribbly three-coloured tapestries but I wanted to push the sewing I was doing in a different direction. Scribbling in the sewn mark is quite beautiful and I wanted to take that and introduce the thickness and richness of oil stick. For the new ones that I'm showing at YSP and at Timothy Taylor, I screen printed my drawings onto the fabric and then sewed over the top, changing the colours here and there. I love getting into the groove with the sewing machine, I like the energy of the process. It's extremely laborious and time-consuming, but I really want them to look quick and spontaneous. I'm calling them thread paintings because they are somewhere between drawing and sewing.

DT: The fabric, which is unstretched, almost looks like crumpled paper.

AM: Exactly. It has a nice unfinished quality. Sometimes things can get too slick, which is why I like things to be very raw, as if they're not quite finished.

DT: What else have you been working on?

AM: I've just completed a commission for Claridge's, it's a bar called the Painter's Room and is the first time in 100 years that the hotel has opened a new bar. I've been working with [the hotelier and owner of Claridge's and Château La Coste] Paddy McKillen on the Château La Coste show and he invited me to do this commission. It's a very small space, only seating about 30 people, and I've decorated the walls with monochrome murals based on my drawings. I wanted to draw directly onto the walls but because it was Claridge's, and I liked the idea of things being more refined, I created this new process where I drew the images, manipulated them on a computer and had them made into vinyl transfers. Then I painted the vinyl with three or four layers of paint so that they have a slightly thick, embossed kind of look. I also took one of my tapestries, which began as a watercolour, and made it into a stained-glass window for the bar. It was really exciting to work with glass and I tried to make it appear like a watercolour painting. The colours look incredible in these beautiful hand-blown pieces of glass.

DT: Is that something you would like to explore further?

AM: Yes, I'd love to make a show of stained glass works. It's a really exciting new direction and I think it could be the next thing for me.

www.studiointernational.com

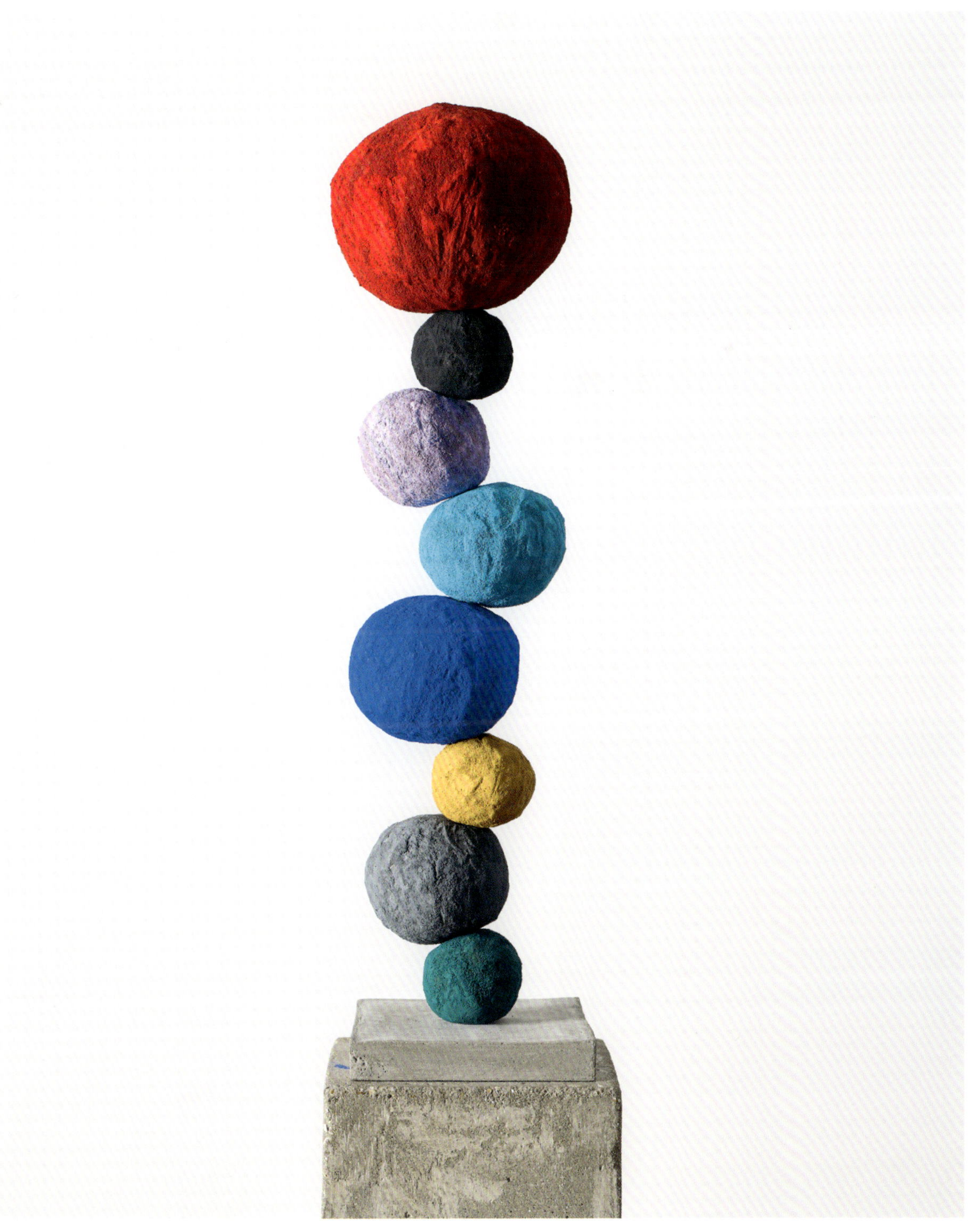

Stack 8, Viridian Green 2021, one of ten sculptures made to support YSP. Photograph Steve White

ARTWORK LIST

Woman with colour 2015, thread on linen canvas
Private Collection, London

Woman with colour 2015, thread on linen canvas
Private Collection, London

Woman with colour 2015, thread on linen canvas
Private Collection, London

Bronze Stack 9, Viridian Green 2017, steel and patinated bronze
Private Collection, London

Stack 2, Copper Blue 2018, foam core, pigment, concrete, steel, plaster, sand
Private Collection, New York

Bronze Stack 9, Cobalt Turquoise 2020, steel and patinated bronze
Private Collection, Texas

Stack 9, Studio Violet 2019, foam core, pigment, concrete, steel, plaster, sand
Private Collection, Paris

Stack 8, Chrome Oxide 2019, foam core, pigment, concrete, steel, plaster, sand
Private Collection, London

Stack 9, Copper Blue 2020, foam core, pigment, concrete, steel, plaster, sand
Private Collection, London

Bronze Stack 9, Ultramarine Blue 2020-21, steel and patinated bronze
Private Collection, New York

Stack 9, Ultramarine Blue 2021, foam core, pigment, concrete, steel, plaster, sand
Private Collection, Hong Kong

Stack 9, Viridian Green 2021, foam core, pigment, concrete, steel, plaster, sand
Private Collection, Madrid

Stack 9, Cobalt Turquoise 2021, foam core, pigment, concrete, steel, plaster, sand
Private Collection, Mumbai

Stack 9, Cobalt Turquoise 2021, foam core, pigment, concrete, steel, plaster, sand
Private Collection, Paris

Stack 3, Cobalt Turquoise 2021, foam core, pigment, concrete, steel, plaster, sand
Private Collection, London

Stack 9, Cadmium Red 2021, foam core, pigment, concrete, steel, plaster, sand
Private Collection, Milan

Stack 8, Viridian Green 2021, foam core, pigment, concrete, steel, plaster, sand
Private Collection, Shanghai

Stack 8, Ultramarine Blue 2021, foam core, pigment, concrete, steel, plaster, sand.
Private Collection, London

Stack 3, Terre Verte 2021, foam core, pigment, concrete, steel, plaster, sand
Private Collection, Istanbul

Night Landscape 2021, thread on cotton.
Private Collection, New York

ANNIE MORRIS SELECTED BIOGRAPHY

1978   Born in England
1997   Studies at Central Saint Martins School of Art and Design, London, UK
1998   Studies at École de Beaux-Arts, Paris, France
2003   Studies at Slade School of Art, London, UK

Selected Solo Exhibitions

2021   *Annie Morris: When a Happy Thing Falls*, Yorkshire Sculpture Park, UK

2021   *Annie Morris*, Timothy Taylor, London, UK

2021   Frieze Sculpture Park, London, UK

2020   *Annie Morris: Diaries* (online), Timothy Taylor, London, UK

2019   *Annie Morris*, Timothy Taylor, New York, NY, USA

                Annie Morris, Union Gallery, London, UK

2018   *New Works*, ProjectB Gallery, Milan, Italy

                Annie Morris: New Work, Winston Wachter Fine Art, New York, NY, USA

2017   *Annie Morris: Cobalt Blue*, Winston Wachter Fine Arts, New York, NY, USA

2015   *Annie Morris: Stacked*, Winston Wachter Fine Art, Seattle, WA, USA

                Ascension, ProjectB Gallery, Milan, Italy

2014   *Annie Morris: Hope From a Thin Line*, Winston Wachter Fine Art, New York, NY, USA

2012   *There Is A Land Called Loss*, Pertwee Anderson and Gold Gallery, London, UK

2010   *Annie Morris*, Winston Wachter Fine Art, New York, NY, USA

2007   *When A Happy Thing Falls*, Allsopp Contemporary Gallery, London, UK

                When A Happy Thing Falls, Jeannie Frielich Contemporary, New York, NY, USA

2006   *Annie Morris*, Lightbox Gallery, Los Angeles, CA, USA

2005   *Annie Morris*, Laura Bartlett Gallery, London, UK

                Annie Morris: Glass Paintings, Postcards, Thomas Williams Gallery, London, UK

2004   *Annie Morris* (curated by Nick Hackworth), The Adams Street Club, London, UK

                The Man With The Dancing Eyes, Daniel Katz Gallery, London, UK

Selected Group Exhibitions

2021	*Colour Space*, Mucciaccia Gallery, Rome, Italy
	London Calling, Fundación Bancaja, Valencia, Spain
2019-2020	*Idris Khan and Annie Morris*, Galerie Isa, Mumbai, India
2018	Astrup Fearnley Museum, Oslo, Norway
	Idris Khan and Annie Morris: Re-Imaginings, Galerie Isa, Mumbai, India
	Surface Work, Victoria Miro, London, UK
2017	*Peter Doig Gala Exhibition*, Whitechapel Gallery, London, UK
	Women and Gluck, The Fine Art Society, London, UK
2015	*After Marcel Duchamp*, The Fine Art Society, London, UK
2014	*The Summer Show*, The Royal Academy, London, UK
2013	*Sculpture Al Fresco III*, Great Fosters Sculpture Park, Surrey, UK
2010	*The House of Fairy Tales*, Tate St Ives, Cornwall, UK

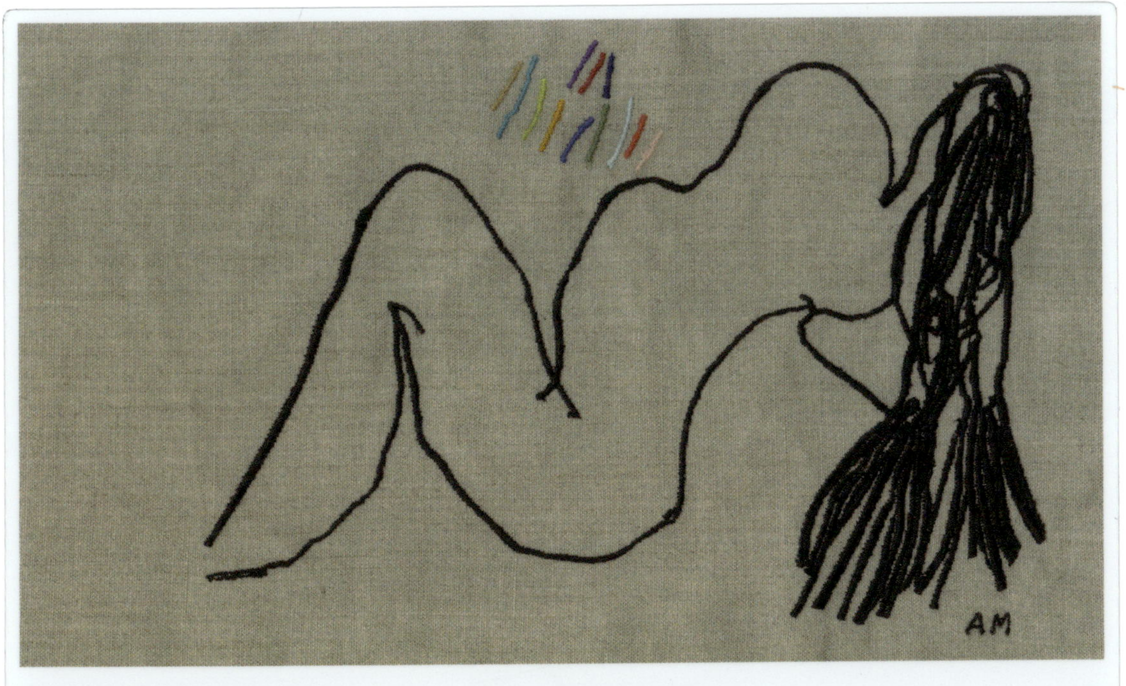

Woman with Colour 2021, thread on linen canvas, edition size 50 + 10 APs
Photograph: Annie Morris studio

COLOPHON

Published by Yorkshire Sculpture Park to accompany
ANNIE MORRIS: WHEN A HAPPY THING FALLS
25 September 2021 to 6 February 2022

Catherine Loewe and YSP texts © the authors and Yorkshire Sculpture Park 2021
Interview with David Trigg © Studio International
All artwork © Annie Morris
ISBN: 978-1-908432-53-7
YSP photography: Jonty Wilde
Retouching: Bérengère Ducoms
Print: Jump North, Sheffield
Proofreading: Eloise Bennett, Kathryn Brame, Sarah Coulson, Emma Spencer,
Charu Vallabhbhai and Kirsty Young

Yorkshire Sculpture Park, West Bretton, Wakefield, WF4 4LG. ysp.org.uk
YSP is an accredited museum and registered charity, number: 1067908

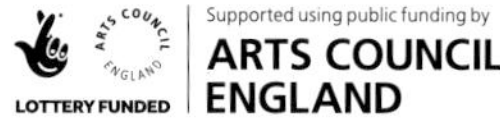
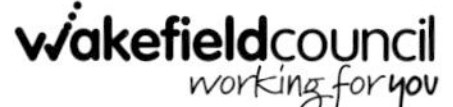